# The Platinum Rainbow

**(How to succeed in the music business
without selling your soul)**

**by**

**Bob Monaco and James Riordan**

*Swordsman Press*
Sherman Oaks, Ca.

*The. Platinum Rainbow*
(how to succeed in the music business without selling your soul)

Published by Swordsman Press
15445 Ventura Blvd., Suite #10
P.O. Box 5973
Sherman Oaks, CA. 91413

1st Printing — December, 1980
2nd Printing — April 1981
3rd Printing — July, 1981
4th Printing — May, 1982
5th Printing — December, 1982
Revised Edition — March, 1983
1st Printing — March 1983
2nd Printing — March 1984
3rd Printing — August 1984

Printed in the U.S.A.

ISBN 0-940018-00-4

Library of Congress Catalog Card No.: 81-126311

# The Authors

Bob Monaco has been in the music business twenty-two years. He has been awarded several Gold and Platinum Albums for his work as a producer with artists such as Chaka Khan & Rufus, Three Dog Night, Carl Carlton, Freda Payne, Tina Turner, Cold Blood, Flora Purim, Airto, Candi Staton, The Sweet Inspirations, Crow and The Cryan' Shames. He also managed The American Breed, Mason Proffit, Flock, Crow, The Cryan' Shames, Rotary Connection featuring the late Minnie Riperton, and was integrally involved with the careers of many other artists including Styx and The Buckinghams. In 1975, as a staff producer for ABC Records, he won a Grammy for the Best R&B Record, "Tell Me Something Good" featuring Chaka Khan & Rufus, and in 1979 he was nominated for another Grammy for Best Latin/Jazz Recording, "Touching You, Touching Me" by Airto.

James Riordan has been in the music business seventeen years. A songwriter and record producer, he is known primarily for writing a nationally syndicated newspaper column on popular music called Rock-Pop. He has written both fiction and non-fiction for many major magazines and his career has included the roles of disc-jockey, agent, performer, concert promoter, and manager. He is currently at work on a screenplay about the music business.

The Platinum Rainbow is used as a text in over a hundred colleges and both authors are very active in the field of education. The Commerical Music Curriculum, which they created, includes a video seminar series featuring professionals from the music industry, artist-in-residence programs, clinics, career counseling, and program counseling for institutions of higher learning across the country. Since the publication of The Platinum Rainbow, Bob Monaco and James Riordan have appeared on numerous national television and radio programs. The response to these appearances has led to the production of both a cable television program and a syndicated radio series which are also entitled "The Platinum Rainbow."

This book is dedicated to our families and friends who for years have had to put up with the incredible aggravation that is a byproduct of our love for the music business, and to the innumerable companies and individuals who have lied to us or misled us in other ways so that we could teach others from our mistakes. Thanks, guys.

# Contents

The Foundation For Your House—Less Is More—
Singing With The Track—Tracking—Overdubs &
Vocals—The $250,000 Toy—The Mix—Picking A
Single—Mastering: Turning Cold Tapes Into Hot
Records

# Introduction:
# Why We Wrote This Book
# In The Way That We Did

As everyone who reads many books may know, the introduction is the place where the author is allowed to dump all of his schmaltzy philosophy on the unsuspecting heads of his readers. It's where writers convince you of how pure their motives are. Usually, the longer the introduction, the purer the motives of the author, or at least that's how it seems. Well, we have some pure motives too. But, like 99 3/4% of everyone who has ever written a book, our prime motivation was income. So, now that you understand that, please allow us to dump all of our schmaltzy philosophy on your somewhat suspecting head, so you know why we wrote this book in the way that we did.

Before we go any further, let's can this ''we'' business. You know that this book is a collaboration of two individuals, but saying ''we'' all the time is awkward and even a little bit tacky. So from now on, ''I'' means either one of us or both of us.

Now that we've got that straight, let's get on to the philosophy. We . . . I mean, I, wrote this book in the way that I did because I wish there had been something like it when I started down the yellow brick road of the music business. It took me a number of years just to find out that I had no idea how this business really worked. Part of the reason for this was that nobody would tell me how it worked, and part of the reason was that I wouldn't listen to anybody who tried. The biggest reason that nobody would tell me how the music business really worked was that nobody really knew. And nobody wants to admit ignorance in a field in which everyone claims to know it all. See Chapter 1,

*"The Mysterious Music Business: Exposing Some Myths"* for more about this area.

While nobody knows all the angles, a person can learn a lot if he keeps his eyes and ears open, and *learns from his mistakes.* Did you notice that this last phrase was in italics? That's because it's important and you can expect to see a lot of it in the coming chapters. You see, I finally learned that learning what you did wrong was the way most people learned how to succeed in the music business. What I hope to do is teach you not to make the same mistakes that I did, and thereby save you a good deal of time. I have used humor to make this book readable, and repetition to drive the message home.

I also want to unmask a few myths about stardom and the music industry. A lot of people get hurt because *they look at the fantasy and not the reality* of the music business. In fact, you could say that Rule Number One is learning to look at the realities. It's possible that, after reading this book, you will decide that you don't want to be part of the business of making records. It may not be worth it to you, and if that's true, then I've still saved you some valuable time and a good deal of pain.

Some of you, however, will go on in your attempt at success or even stardom, no matter what I or anyone else says to you about how crazy and difficult this business is to succeed in. That's good! In fact, that is exactly what it takes. The difference between those who attain success and those who do not is quite often that *those who failed gave up first.* It is my desire to teach you some of the ground rules and as many of the angles as I have been able to learn, so that when you're finished with this book you can see the reality through all the garbage, learn from your mistakes, have a general plan, and create your own angles. And if my purest motivation is attained, you should have some idea of how to feel good about yourself through the ups and downs. I'm no preacher and I'm no shrink, but I can tell you that you've got to be a success on the inside before being one on the outside makes any real difference. There . . . was that schmaltzy enough for you? Okay, let's get on with the show.

# Preface
# What This Book Will And Won't Do For You

*"One of the things that makes the music business a crazy business is that it is such a young business. And because it is such a young business, there are no rules."*
**—David Crosby** *

In case you're wondering why this book has an introduction *and* a preface, when you thought they were the same thing, it's because I wanted to introduce my motives, or what this book will do for me, and I wanted to comment on what this book will do for you. Also, I decided that the difference between an introduction and a preface is that an introduction goes first (decided, like most important things in this world, by the flip of a 1974 Lincoln penny).

First of all, let's get one thing straight. This book won't make you a success. Only you can do that. In fact, if you're naive enough to believe reading a book can make you a success, don't even read this book, because you won't understand it anyway. Instead, wait for my book on "How To Buy Land On The Other Side Of The Moon."

While I'm at it, remember that all the jive you hear about an important music business executive making someone a success is just that—jive. Nobody makes anybody a success, and nobody is going to do it for you. No matter how powerful a manager, agent or producer you may know, he can only open doors for

* © *Rock-Pop 10/23/75*

you. It's still you who has to go out on that stage, or into that studio, or wherever your gig takes place, and make it happen. You must realize at all times that it is what you do when you're "on" and how well you do it that makes or breaks you. If you're a songwriter, then you're "on" when you're sitting in front of the piano or holding the guitar. If you're a producer, you're "on" when you walk into the studio. If you're a manager, you're "on" when you go into your rap. It's the moment when you have to shine, and no one recognizes it better than you.

This book is primarily designed for people who want to become successful recording artists. But to be a successful manager, producer, publicist, or agent, you must know how, to some extent, to make someone else a successful recording artist. In addition to this, there are special sections devoted to becoming a successful manager, producer, publicist, agent, songwriter, engineer, record label executive, and publisher. Basically, if you want to be involved in the music business, you should read this book.

Besides the above reasons, you have to *make yourself a success* because you won't be able to get a manager (or a job) that has the power to open real doors for you, until you do. This may sound like a Catch-22 or the old chicken/egg game, but it's true, nevertheless. To get a top manager or other first rate music business person to take you on as a client or an employee, you have to develop yourself to the point where you're already a success in every area but your bankbook. You have to be able to impress someone who may be so jaded that if you could combine the seven wonders of the world into one stage show, they would say something like, "Well, it's not bad, but of course, you know it needs a lot of work."

But don't get discouraged. Remember that someone turned down the Beatles because he didn't think they would sell. Sure, there were reasons which, at the time, made as much sense as the reasons you get rejected today. They said the Beatles sounded too much like the Everly Brothers or Chuck Berry. Others probably said they didn't sound enough like the Everly Brothers or Chuck Berry. Obviously, they were wrong. The execs who turned down the Beatles made the same mistake that every other exec has made at one time or another. They allowed themselves to be conditioned to say "no" more than they allowed themselves to recognize true potential. The point is that nobody knows it all (see Chapter 1—*"Exposing Some Myths—The Golden Reel to Reel and The Platinum Turntable"*). You can, and may, get a hundred "no" answers, but it only takes one "yes." So don't get discouraged, and don't ever lose sight of your goal.

This book will show you what you need to do to give "making it in the music business" your best shot—the steps you must go through to create, develop, polish, perfect, and market your act. And your "act" can include anything from your job qualifications, to your songs, your recorded sound, your visual appeal, your live show, and your business savvy. It's how to hone your edge. This book won't give you talent you don't have, but it will teach you how to develop and direct the talent you already possess.

One more word on managers. This book is not a substitute for a good manager, but it will show you how to work along with the power and clout of a manager. (Clout is a term you will hear a lot in the music business. Everyone wants it because no one has enough of it. Clout is roughly equivalent to owning Boardwalk, Park Place, and all the railroads in Monopoly. The way some guys play, it's owning Free Parking, Chance, Community Chest, and the Bank as well. You think I'm kidding, don't you? Some people won't even play the game unless you give them all that and more, before they roll the dice and they *still* get mad if they lose!)

Another thing this book won't do for you is enable you to totally escape those experiences which we in the music business term as "rotten." There is really no escaping a few bad experiences, but it need not be as bad as you've heard. Hopefully, you will learn how to minimize the bummers* that you have to go through, and recognize when one is on the way. While you will have to endure a few bad experiences, you can learn enough from each mistake to keep from repeating it somewhere down the line. A lot of folks in this business repeat the same

---

*bummer* is defined by the *"Jefferson Airplane Handbook To Genuine Rock Jargon"* as a bad experience; sometimes, but not always, associated with drugs.

mistakes over and over again throughout their entire career. Bad experiences can happen at both a very low level or a very high level in terms of how close you are to attaining your goals. It's better to learn to deal with the bummers at a lower level, than to get near the top and have your balloon burst. Knowing the realities of this business can make all the difference between those alternatives.

I can't guarantee that you will escape the queasy feeling that occurs simultaneously in your head and stomach when you discover something like your manager splitting town with all the money from the big gig. But I can teach you how to really know the people you work with before you trust them. I can also help you recognize and deal with experiences which may be more subtle, but just as devastating in the long run.

Don't think that all bad experiences are caused by making a mistake, because some of them just happen. There is a popular misconception that succeeding in the music business is about 10% knowledge and 90% luck. That's not true. It's more like 15% knowledge and 85% luck. Seriously, it's probably closer to fifty-fifty, but whatever the ratio, you can determine your success by knowing how to make your own breaks and, equally important, by knowing how to recognize and take advantage of the ones that do come your way.

Another thing that will measure both how soon you attain success and how well you adjust to it is your recovery time. There's a nasty tendency in this business to fall rather than roll with the punches. Sometimes people are so depressed over a turndown or some other kind of disappointment that they literally can't function properly for *months*. And sometimes they become walking tombstones and never get it together quite the way they once had it. It's very sad to think that they might have succeeded if they had walked into one more office or made one more phone call. Then again, they might not ever have "made it"; but realistically, it goes back to recognizing what is going on inside your head. If you aren't doing things quite as efficiently as you used to, ask yourself why. If you're avoiding calling someone, ask yourself why. If you can't seem to find time to accomplish a simple task like having a tape copied, ask yourself why.

You'll be surprised at how often the answer is connected with fear. Usually it's the *fear of rejection* that keeps you from giving your best effort. Consciously you have made the decision to risk rejection in the hopes of attaining success, but subconsciously that fear can still hold you back. You don't have to be a psychologist to overcome this area of your subconscious. All you have to do is be able to objectively check yourself out. Just resolve that whenever you find an apparently groundless fear holding you back (like fear of rejection), you will overcome it and do what is right in that situation. This alone will save you an unbelievable amount of time.

In many ways, a career in the music business is very much like a relationship with a woman. In both things you are dealing with a mixture of fantasy and reality, and both are usually complicated by intense desire. So you have ups and downs, needless anxiety, pain, unpredictability, and often bitter disappointment, but always the promise of an exciting victory. After a while, it becomes very difficult to separate yourself from your career and it starts to seem as though *any* time that is not spent in pursuing the dream is just wasted time. The sooner you see through this fallacy, the sooner you will be able to enjoy the segment of your life that is not directly concerned with pursuing success.

It is important to remember that this business has no love for you, no matter how much love you have for it. Success here is measured rather coldly, but purely, in terms of dollars. The big picture is not how big a success you become, but what all this does for you inside. I know people who sell half a million records and are miserable because they don't sell a million. And it's not limited to the artists. I know businessmen who are making seventy-five grand and are depressed because they are not making a hundred. Money and fame give you power, and power gives you a certain degree of freedom in practicing your career, but if you wind up feeling like a piece of garbage packed inside a white satin suit, then it just wasn't worth it. To really succeed, you've got to come out feeling good about yourself and about what you do.

Artists and business successes influence and motivate people for better or worse, and there's a certain responsibility in that.

So you have a responsibility both to yourself and to those whom you influence. What that means is that you have to try to do your best. It doesn't mean, however, that you have to be perfect. Some very successful people in this business are unhappy because somewhere down the line they got the words "success" and "perfection" mixed up with each other. To be a true success you don't have to be perfect, but you do have to be at least a little bit happy. For more on this, consult your local Beverly Hills psychologist.

So now you are ready to plunge headfirst into the music business. That is unless you are already in up to your neck and are reading this book to see how you can keep afloat. In the following chapters you will find a rough step-by-step guide to attaining success in the music business. It is not exactly step-by-step, because there are so many side-steps that you must conquer, and because there is no single route to success. There are a variety of paths, but you still can't go from "A" to "Z" without hitting all the letters in between. You don't want to leapfrog, because you might miss something that you really need further down the line. There's no magic to this business. The closest thing to magic is the creative process which, despite the myth, can be improved and developed with practice. So plunge on. Expect peaks and valleys, and be content to go one step at a time. And remember, there are no rules, not even the ones we tell you about in this book.

# Chapter 1
# The Mysterious Music Business:
# Exposing Some Myths

*"Just remember one thing. Whatever level you're on, it's going to be the same bullshit. The people that are dishing it out just change costumes, that's all. At the bottom, the guy's got an apron on, and maybe he's selling beer at the club you're working at. At the top, it's the president of some exotic record company. They're still feeding you the same doo-doo."*

**Frank Zappa***

One of the things that makes it so difficult to succeed in the music business is all the mystery and myth that surrounds anything as romantic as stardom. Even if you don't want to be a star and would be content with just making a decent living, you still have to focus on reality. And focusing on reality means seeing through some of the popular myths. I've picked out some of the more treacherous, with the hope that you'll soon understand how to spot them on your own. Hint: most of the myths usually have to do with the rock n' roll fairytale. You know the one. The lousy singer is getting nowhere fast when his fairy

* ©Rock-Pop 4/10/77

godfather appears in a three hundred dollar suit with a silk shirt and a little gold spoon around his neck. The fairy godfather waves his magic wand (a rolled-up record contract) and poof! A new star is born. Well, I don't want to bust your rock n' roll balloon, but that just ain't how it is.

## MYTH NUMBER ONE: The Golden Reel To Reel & The Platinum Turntable

There he is. Your first big-time music business executive. After spending the two hours in his reception room memorizing the Billboard charts for that week, in the hope that this will somehow help you talk shop if the occasion arises, you are told by an incredibly attractive girl, who is wearing $40 jeans and $95 shoes, that you may go in. The ten cups of coffee begin to take effect, and you wish you either hadn't gotten loaded at all, or else had gotten more loaded so you wouldn't care. You step through the door and you are instantly blinded. As you fall into a chair that is too low and too far away from the desk, you recover your sight and realize that you were "gold blind" for a moment. This is a common problem in the recording field, and results from the afternoon sun reflecting off an entire wall of gold records. Having fully recovered, you are shocked to see how friendly the man behind the desk appears to be. As you watch him put your tape on and listen to his concerned questions and clever comments, you feel relieved. This is much nicer than you expected. In fact, this man is so nice, you can't imagine him saying no. (Don't worry, you'll be able to imagine it soon enough.)

The first hint you receive that the nice man may not be too receptive to your material is when he pushes the fast-forward button three seconds into the first song. He stops the tape in time to hear the only place you sing flat on the entire demo, and then pauses to say something like, "I kind of like what you're into, but I don't think you've quite found it yet." But because he is so nice, he goes ahead and listens to almost seven full seconds of the third song before taking the tape off. He then tells you to develop your act, band, or songs a little more, and to feel free to see him again.

Back on the street, your first thought is that you should quit and give up on this crazy dream that everyone told you would be exactly like it is, even though you won't admit that to anyone. Your second thought is to do whatever it was the nice man told you to do with your music, assuming that it isn't obscene. Your third thought is one of hope, because perhaps the nice man will see you again when you have made a new tape. But the thought that matters, and the one that gets you to the next interview, is that perhaps the nice man didn't quite give your tape the attention he should have, and as a result, may not know what the hell he is talking about.

There are some people who lay their cards on the table, and the rest pretend to lay their cards on the table. The *Golden Reel To Reel & The Platinum Turntable Myth* is the belief that people in positions of power in this business are rarely wrong. The truth is that they are rarely right. They keep their jobs by playing the percentages effectively, and that means being right now and then, but it does not mean they are infallible. May I remind you once again of those sorry souls who turned down the Beatles. If John Lennon had believed in the *G.R.T.R.& T.P.T. Myth,* he would never have made it over to Brian Epstein's office where, as they say, the rest is history. The same is true for any superstar. Everyone gets turned down a whole lot before they get a yes. But it only takes one yes to do the trick. I remember one time when I had seen so many publishers I could not imagine one being able to pronounce the word "yes." I was looking at this guy across the desk while he was listening to my tape and trying to imagine how he would say it. Would he say "Let's do it," or "I'll take these," or "What kind of a deal do you want?" or what? I was still trying to figure it out when he said, "I'll publish these songs." My first thought was how simple it is when it is right. And that's how it is, no matter what you are trying to sell, and no matter who you are trying to sell it to.

The reasons people act as though they have a golden reel to

reel or a platinum turntable is that this is a business where nobody has half the answers, but everybody likes to think they know it all. It stands to reason that in an industry where those with the big ego are the ones who usually survive, everyone will have an "important" opinion.

Despite the constant effort at formulating the hit record, no one has invented a machine that, upon hearing your record, will move a needle to the categories of dud, miss, hit, and monster. But there are a lot of people who like to pretend they have such machines built inside their head. This uncanny ability to recognize a hit upon first listening is called "ears" and almost nobody really has them. The few people who do have great ears usually won't tell you about it. Anyone who starts rapping to you about having "the best ears in the business" probably couldn't tell a hit record from a shotput.

The important thing is to remember that this business is built on a variety of tastes. No matter what someone's track record is at picking hits, he may not be able to recognize your potential, simply because your music is not compatible with his particular taste. The opinions are always going to be there, but the one that matters most is yours. The taste that you should believe in is your own. If you feel really strong about a particular song, and "the people who count" (A&R men, Managers, Producers, and Publishers, for example) give you the wrong reaction, you have to be strong enough to do what you think is best. If you allow yourself to be swayed by every "professional" that you meet, you will wind up sounding like a cross between early Frank Zappa and late Spike Jones—a bunch of strange noise. You can't please everybody. The trick is to know when you please yourself.

Constructive criticism is a different matter. In order to develop your music, you've got to be able to screen any criticism for the elements in it that may be constructive. You can be very open-minded and listen to a lot of things, but it's how you let them affect you that counts. Generally, constructive criticism comes from a well-respected peer who is sincerely concerned about what you are doing. Whenever someone listens to your music and offers his suggestions, screen them according to the following guidelines: 1) Does the person know what they are talking about? 2) Are they concerned with your welfare? 3) Does their own taste prevent them from relating to your music? 4) Have others expressed a similar opinion? 5) Will the proposed changes be worth the difficulty in making them? 6) Are you listening to what the person is saying because it makes sense, or because they are supposed to be important? This list can go on and on in order to fit special cases, but you get the idea.

The way to overcome the *G.R.T.R. & T.P.T. Myth* is not to let yourself be intimidated by fancy offices, gold records, power, and prestige. Above all, don't allow yourself to get thrown off the right track by someone behind a desk. Remember, a lot of these people are *crazy*. No single opinion matters that much and this business functions by hit and miss. They throw a lot of stuff out there and see what hits. It all depends on what grabs them. If it doesn't grab one guy, it may grab another across the street.

Before we go on to Myth Number Two, I'll tell you a true story with the names changed (so I don't get sued) to illustrate my point. A long time ago in Nashville, I had a song that I thought was perfect for a big name, middle-of-the-road artist. I took a tape of songs which included this tune to the song plugger for the artist's publishing company, who I shall call Joey Smith. Joey listened to the tape and said he didn't hear anything that was right for them or the name artist in particular. I asked him specifically about the song I believed in, but he said no. I left and went across the street and played the same tape for a guy named Bobby at a different publishing company. Bobby stopped the tape when he heard the song in question, jumped up and dramatically announced, "Joey Smith will love that song." I told Bobby that I just played it for Joey and he didn't like it. "He'll love it," Bobby persisted. "Let's go over and play it for him right now." I told him I was just there, but he said not to worry about that, and before long, we were back in Joey Smith's office. Bobby told him about the song, and Joey said, "Well, let's hear it," and put the exact same tape back on his machine which he had played only a half hour before. I reminded him of that, but he didn't pay any attention. When the song played, he said, "I do like that. I'm sure that _____ (the big name middle-of-the-road artist) will love it." I asked him why he didn't like the song a half hour ago, and he just said, "I couldn't hear it as a hit then, but now I hear it. I like it a lot." Bobby published the song, but before anything happened, he left the company and my song was stuck with another publisher who couldn't "hear" it either. Joey, by the way, has written several big country and pop hits. The point is that no one knows all the answers and these people change their opinions like most people change socks.

## MYTH NUMBER TWO: "Waiting To Be Discovered"

A lot of bands are, at this moment, playing in some bar in the Midwest, hoping that Robert Stigwood is going to pop in for a drink. If not Stigwood, then maybe someone else whose job is scouting out new talent for a record company. Well, it just isn't done that way anymore. Playing at Gala Lanes is not going to get you a record contract. No "Brian Epstein" is going to bop in and make you the next Beatles (In fact, Brian Epstein was one of the last people to check out unknown bands in unknown clubs.) Nobody is going to come to you. Even if you're gigging at the hot showcase clubs in L.A., you can't depend on anyone from a record label being there unless you personally get their commitment to see the show. A & R men just don't look for acts in out-of-the-way clubs anymore. Why should they, when they've got groups on their doorstep with master quality tapes to present. With a quality demo, the A & R man doesn't have to worry if the band will freeze up in the studio or what they'll sound like on record. All he has to do is decide if he likes it.

After you decide you want to make your living from music, one of the next things to decide is the specific career you want to pursue. Do you want to be an agent, a concert promoter, a singer, a songwriter, a publicist, a critic, a producer, a recording artist, a nightclub performer, or what? If you want to be a recording artist, then you must realize that making your living by playing clubs is a different game. If you want to play clubs, that's great, but recognize your chances (old reality again) in regard to a recording career. You can play every bowling alley in Iowa, but don't expect anything to happen beyond getting good tour experience and improving your hook (your bowling hook, not your songwriting hook). Don't make the mistake of saying, "We'll play clubs for a while until we're ready to make the demo, and go for it," unless you have a definite plan and are prepared to stick to it. I know four zillion bands that had that same idea and wound up just another bar band. What happens is the old best-laid-plans-of-mice-and-men routine. After a while, you get used to the club money coming in and you spend it. And you get a little wasteful and pretty soon you have to put off the demo. And then everybody's so burned out, you take a little vacation and put off the demo again. And then the drummer's wife has a baby and you buy a new guitar, and pretty soon you can't quit the road for anything. Then you become like this one band I knew in Illinois. They were tight and consistently blew away the crowds in the local bars. They were playing all over the Midwest, and they had developed a strong stage act. The only problem was they worked on their original songs for a half hour on Sunday afternoons, and it sounded like it. They were waiting for someone to see their act and be so knocked out that they would put up enough money to not only cover studio expenses, but pay everybody's bills while they got the demo together. All this with no original tunes in the act.

After about five years at this stage, if the band doesn't break up, they become a "punch-in" band. They punch in at 8 and quit at 2. Gee, isn't that great? Just like a factory, except you don't get an hour for lunch. And instead of working on machines all day, you get to play songs you hate all night. At this point, most bands just give up all hope of ever landing a record deal without ever really giving it a shot. That's fine, if that's what you want. Playing bars can be a nice life once you get used to it, but while you're there, don't kid yourself about your chances at the big time.

Actually, playing clubs to *develop* your act is the best way to go, and the week or two nightclub gigs are great for trying things out. If you plan it out and everybody agrees on some sort of timetable or step-by-step program, then it's worth the effort. But don't let your original tunes or arrangements suffer. And don't fall into the trap of playing local rock n' roll star. You know the guy. Leaps on stage, cranks up his amp, pretends to be Peter Townshend all night, and makes it with every cocktail waitress on the circuit. That's cute, but in the words of P.T. Barnum, "It ain't gonna make you no star." Actually, P.T. Barnum never said that, but what did he know about rock n' roll anyway?

One more caution about playing clubs, and this is particularly directed to the ladies—beware of the *"friend of a friend."* The *"friend of a friend"* is a fast-growing species whose habitat is primarily small cocktail lounges, but they have been known to frequent concert clubs as well. Their most sought-after prey, however, is the female solo artist who performs nightly at one Holiday Inn or another. The male of the species can be recognized easiest by his unique call, which is different variations of the phrase, "I really think you have the talent to be a big star" and "I have a friend who is big in the music business." Physically, the *"friend of a friend"* seems to be forever forty, a little to a lot on the chubby side, and in the insurance or traveling sales business. The most common method of capturing victims involves luring the prey up to the nest for a discussion and a nightcap. Inevitably the *"friend of a friend"* will promise to make an important phone call the next day, which inevitably either never happens or doesn't amount to much. The *"friend of a friend"* may also carry a camera and volunteer to shoot publicity shots or some such nonsense. The female of the species is somewhat less imaginative, and is usually only a *"friend of a friend"* of someone who is rich. While rare instances have produced tangible results, the *"friend of a friend"* should be viewed with extreme caution.

Obviously, the way to resolve the "Waiting To Be Discovered" myth is not to wait. Take steps to be heard. More will be discussed about this, but remember that it is often easier to get someone to listen to a tape than to drag your whole band down to some club and perform, hoping that the person shows up. You've got to take control over the situation and not wait for anybody to discover you. You have to discover them first and make them interested. The idea is to take positive action for your own cause.

### MYTH NUMBER THREE: "We Don't Want To Do Gigs, We'll Just Make Records" or "Everybody Wants To Be Steely Dan."

While playing gigs may not get you discovered, it's a cinch that you must have your stage act down to get a record deal. This will be covered in depth in a later chapter, but there seem to be more and more bands who, frustrated by the hassles of playing small-time gigs, decide they are going to be a "recording band." If what you mean by recording band is a band who is trying to get their recorded sound together first, that's fine, as long as you realize that at some point you must master the stage and learn how to win over an audience. The myth is that new bands can get away without doing gigs. They can't—not by a long shot. The first thing the record company is going to say after they've decided they like your tape is, where can they see you play? And that is not the time to start worrying about a live show. I realize that playing gigs for many bands means learning a lot of horrible Top 40 songs which you may consider a waste of time. But, learning these songs can be a positive thing if you look at it that way. You are learning more about the public's taste. Not their general taste—that you can hear on the radio. It's the little things that make a song a hit which become clearer to you when you study them. A particular riff, a background harmony, and a unique drum roll, are things that you can later weave into your own sound and build on—making the knowledge very valuable. But the big value is learning how to take charge on stage. It you feel that you simply can't do that playing hit dance tunes in the local club, then you'd better pack up the band and split to somewhere else. You have to build and test your stage show in front of an audience before you can expect to get a record deal.

One of the biggest reasons for the fall of disco is the lack of good, live performances. They made a lot of great records, but the artists couldn't cut it on stage. The records were primarily made by the producers, and the artists weren't really developed. You can only have so many black girls in gold lame' pants with head crowns and butterflies on their rear end. The live show is *very* important to develop.

The only bands who make records without touring to sell those records are bands that are big enough to afford it. And almost all of them started out touring like crazy when they got their first record deal. When you've been a part of two or three top bands, then you can decide you're going to make records without playing gigs, but until you're at that level, don't even entertain the thought. A record label will drop you like a cement tennis ball if they hear you have an aversion to doing gigs. There's enough going against you without buying into this myth and adding to your problems.

### MYTH NUMBER FOUR: "You Won't Succeed If You Don't Know The Biz Inside And Out" or "Thinking You Have To Memorize Billboard."

There are an extraordinary number of people who, each week, sit down and read the "Trades" from cover to cover, with the cockeyed idea that knowing about RCA's new distribution deal in Bolivia somehow might help them get a record deal. Knowing what's going on is impossible in the complete sense, and most of the time it's not worth knowing, since it changes every two weeks anyway. Sure, you should be aware of industry trends, but not to the point where it takes time away from the development of your act. In the same sense your manager should be on the phone hustling for you, not playing with the stock quotations. Knowing the biz in the absolute sense is like trying to be familiar with every name that could help your career. I tried to do that once. I tried to memorize all the execs and departments at Atlantic Records. That was the first label I did because it started with "A" and I gave up after about ten folks. There are so many important people in this business that no accurate "Who's Who" could even begin to be compiled. First of all, you've got every member of every rock band, and each of their attorneys. All the managers, producers, top engineers, and publishers. Then you've got all the heavies who own the big studios, and all their attorneys. You can't forget the agents, promotors, and the fine people who own and manage the important venues in this country and the world. Then you should know the people who own the showcase clubs, and don't forget the top graphics people, the road managers, and the tour coordinators. Now all you've got left is the press, the press agents, the entire radio population, and every executive at every record level. And when you've got all that down, you can start on the attorney's attorneys and, by that time, it's time to start over because so many new people have broken in.

The important thing is not to be sucked in by Myth Number Four. Don't worry about all the things you don't know. Just worry about getting your act together. The rest will come even if you don't know what constitutes a gold record in Finland. You've got to trim the fat in this business, because it's loaded with it. In fact, once you start looking with a discerning eye, you begin to wonder if there is any meat, but believe me, there's enough to keep you plenty busy. So stop being intimidated by what you don't know, and start learning the things that are important. Who cares if you can't talk shop effectively. Nobody else can, either, and besides, if someone isn't interested in you because you didn't hear about some big radio station switching from disco to new wave, you don't want to work with them anyway. If anyone ever puts you down for being ignorant about some industry gossip, tell them you've been too busy working on your music to pay much attention. The idea is not letting knowledge about the state of the business become the trees that keep you from seeing the forest.

**MYTH NUMBER FIVE: "The Best Way To Get Contacts Is To Party With The Stars; Therefore, You Should Party With The Stars Whenever Possible."**

It is true that meeting people is an important part of attaining success in the music business. And it is also true that important people tend to travel in their own circles and it's usually only by hanging around with them that you get to meet others. But this needs to be qualified somewhat, because in Hollywood today you have people who literally do nothing but hang around with important people, hoping to advance their careers. This is fine in some cases, but often the careers get sidetracked into just hanging around.

Going to an exclusive Hollywood party is not that big a deal, and does almost nothing for your career. First of all, anyone who is truly important enough to help your career probably does not want to meet you, and hanging around and acting nonchalant deals a low blow to your self-respect. The problem with making contacts is that everyone tries to connect with someone ten rungs up the ladder, which is almost impossible. The way to make parties and the like work for you is to concentrate on connecting with people to whom you can be mutually beneficial, even though it may not mean an inside lane to the president of Warners. Oftentimes, a guy who will fix your microphone for a reasonable fee is more beneficial to you than the head of Warners could be at that point in your career anyway. It's up to you to know that, and that means *being aware of reality* again. It's funny how often that comes up, isn't it? That's because any business which is built on selling fantasies and contrived images as much as this one is, has got to have "identifying reality" as one of its biggest problems.

Another result of this problem is the amazing amount of time people in this business spend pretending to be somebody. Without any doubt whatsoever, I can truthfully state that I know some individuals who could really *be* somebody if they could successfully channel half the energy they spend *pretending* to be somebody. I used to go to every Hollywood or music bizz party that I could, and tell myself that I was doing it to make the necessary contacts. The real reason I was doing it was to pretend that I was somebody, because the frustration of being nobody is so depressing. At one of those parties where "everybody is important," I could get a whole lot of admiring glances, especially if I dressed the part, which of course I always did. I even developed a way of answering questions that implied I was somebody terribly important, by down-playing the situation. Example: A half-drunk woman comes up to me and, noticing my rock star clothes (rich, but not too neat), says, "You play guitar, don't you?" I answer, "Not very well," and nod as I move into the crowd. For the rest of the night she wonders if I'm Eric Clapton.

It works best if there are two of you playing the game. Then, whenever someone says something like, "I know you from somewhere, don't I?" you can look knowingly at your friend and say, "I don't think so," or if they say, "I've seen your picture before, haven't I?" you can again look knowingly at your friend and reply, "Possibly." The key is to always act like you are mildly amused by everything, while appearing to be ready to leave at any moment. You just have to keep moving enough to avoid specific questions which would force you to lie. Appear vaguely mysterious and equally reluctant to be pinned down. It helps sometimes to be able to look as though you don't want anyone to recognize you, but this takes time to develop. You can't just wear dark glasses or hide your face in your coat every time someone stares at you.

You see how it gets. Just pretending to be someone can become a whole science, and if you think I'm exaggerating, pop into one of the "in" places and watch the crowd. The only thing anybody is concerned about is who is looking at them, and whether the person across the room is really somebody, or just a better jiver than they are. You can get a whole lot farther by staying home and practicing the guitar, or writing new songs, or just listening to records, than you can by pretending to be Neil Young's kid brother. Believe it or not, this also applies to people who aspire to be record executives. You may want to be a publicist, or in A & R, or promotion, or whatever, and it's true that you have to mingle better than your average rock star. But again, the trick is recognizing when you're helping your career and when you're just getting drunk. It's a damn shame that ass-kissing often succeeds in this business, and without the right perspective, it not only hurts your career, but destroys you as a human being.

## MYTH NUMBER SIX: "The Creative Process Is So Fragile That You Have No Control Over It."

This is a myth which seems to plague established stars as much or even more than those still knocking at the door. It is true for some people, but usually only for those who grew up believing it. You won't burn out from the inside unless you first burn out from the outside. The ideas don't just stop. The songs don't stop coming unless you set up a block and the block that most people create is brought about by heavy drinking and drugs. The whole body wears down and finally the creative process goes with it.

This does not mean that everyone should be able to write a song on cue or come up with the perfect marketing plan for an album between noon and two p.m. Most people have their own best ways to create and it is a rare person who can crank it out all the time. But it's going to the other extreme to believe that you can't work for results. Often the only way you get that perfect hook is to keep pounding away at the piano until you find it. You've got to know when to work for it and when to wait for it to come. In general, however, the delicacy of the creative process is underestimated by record labels and over-estimated by artists. It's easy to justify laziness as artistic license, but remember that if you get too lazy, it won't be art that you are producing any more. There are few things as unartistic as an artist who has screwed off for an entire year, and ten days before the deadline, decides he will stock up on coke and speed, and wait for some spontaneous creativity. It happens sometimes, but it gets harder all the time.

## MYTH NUMBER SEVEN: "To Be Successful, You Must Learn How To Be Commercial."

I have this friend who has been in a very tight rock band for about three years now. The band is very good, but they keep changing their name and their music to fit in with the current trend. They are working way too hard at sounding commercial. Before the right people get to hear them, they decide they aren't "happening anymore" or else somebody who is nobody gives them some crazy advice and they change everything around again. When I first heard them, they sounded very unique, comparable perhaps to "Supertramp," but very few others. On the advice of a struggling young manager, who supposedly knew what was happening, even though he had been unable to make it pay (there really are a few such people, but not very many), they changed their vocal style and shifted away from keyboard to guitar. They wound up sounding like "Foreigner." This lasted until they got a new "producer" who wanted them to get into new wave. They did, of course, and besides cutting their hair to look the part, they changed their music and vocal style *again* on the advice of someone they barely knew. This time they came out sounding like "The Cars." Having been without a manager or producer for the last few months, the group has now shifted into their own hard rock/new wave blend, which sounds pretty good. But the odds are that they will change that as soon as someone "advises" them.

You have to be sure of yourself. There is no such thing as being commercial, because anything that sells is, by definition, commercial. While it is desirable to have strong hook lines in your songs and not sound so off-the-wall that no one can relate to you, it doesn't make any sense to change your sound with every new hit that climbs the charts. You have to like your sound and have enough confidence in it to know that a lot of other people will like it too. Don't get so caught up in playing the music business game that you forget about the general public. If *they* like you, you can find a record company that likes you too. The public still buys the records, even though they usually buy what they hear on the radio. The point is that you can't try to sound commercial. It comes out too forced, rigid, and uninspired. What you can do is find your own style and then put a few touches on it to make it more accessible. It's pointless to try to change your style to fit the latest trend because by the time you master it, there will be a new trend.

If you've got a particular strength and direction, go with it. If you love to perform country music and that's where you feel comfortable, then do it. Don't sell out to disco because disco is in. Don't try to become funky if it's not in your blood. A lot of publishers will try to teach you how to write "commercial." A very few of them give out sound (pardon the pun) advice. A lot of these guys just have a hangup about being part of the creative process. Trying to be commercial can really screw you up. A lot of artists aren't doing *anything* in their chosen field because they feel they can never be commercial. Don't worry about being commercial, just worry about being good!

## MYTH NUMBER EIGHT: "Record Companies Know What They're Looking For."

This would be true is you added "once they have found it" to the axiom. That is the problem. A label looks for something that is unique, but accessible. What is unique? Well, one thing that is unique is really having your act together. If you have strong songs, good presentation, and the right look, you're unique. If you have a great lead singer, a hot guitar player, a cookin' bass player, and a kickass drummer who all work well together, that is also unique. It can be almost any combination of these and other things, but usually it all has to happen at the same time. It is a hard thing to pin down, which is why mastering the basics is so important. More on this in a later chapter, but remember that being very professional at what you do and developing your sound (until it doesn't sound like anyone else) is the way to start.

## MYTH NUMBER NINE: "The Music Business Is Controlled By a) Gangsters, b) Jews or c) Attorneys and Accountants."

This is a very popular myth among parents who want to discourage their kids from wasting away in the music business, but that, unfortunately, is not where it stops. I hear all three laments quite frequently from people who should know better. Taking them one by one, there is no denying that there is an element of organized crime present in the music business. Any business that has the high profit margin that the record business does will attract syndicate influence. But that does not mean you have to sell out to the mob to get an album out. Some of the money behind certain companies and individuals may come from the proceeds of organized crime, but it's highly unlikely you'll be exposed to it.

Part B obviously comes from anti-Jewish factions and should be ignored on the grounds of race prejudice alone. Nonetheless, you hear it a lot. I can remember when I was little, hearing my family doctor rattle off the names of every Jewish entertainer he knew, as a warning to me that I didn't have a chance in this business unless I was Jewish. This, of course, is not true. After changing my name to Goldberg for five years and realizing it didn't help my career, I changed it back.

Part C is probably closer to the truth than parts A and B, but it is also false. Many labels seem to act as though their actions were controlled by accountants and attorneys, but this is not entirely the case. There are some music business attorneys who are among the most powerful individuals in the industry, but they certainly don't function as a clique (more about attorneys later). If the music business is controlled by any group, it is by big business, which, after all, controls everything else, so why let it bother you?

## MYTH NUMBER TEN: "A Record Deal Means Success!"

Wrong. This is the most popular of all the myths that I've mentioned. Everyone seems to think they'll have it made if they can just get that record contract. It isn't true. Most people have no idea how many deals never get to be albums, how many albums never get released, how many releases never get heard, and how many that are heard never sell. Ask anyone who's had a record out and they'll tell you that it's just one more step on the ladder. Granted, it is a very big step and a very difficult one to make, but it doesn't mean you've won the game. Having a signed contract only means that you are first and ten on the forty yard line. You've got a long way to go to get across that goal line, but at least you're in the game. You're definitely giving it a real shot. Having a record deal takes you from the amateur ranks and puts you in with the professionals. Like most dreams, the closer you come to achieving it, the more you realize it isn't the way you thought it was at all. So, don't sell your soul for a record deal, because it may not mean that much in the long run.

# Chapter 2
# Are You Serious?

*"In order to accomplish anything you have to make some kind of commitment. That should be part of everyone's attitude. There has to be a point at which you stand for your beliefs, and that requires making a serious effort."*
**—Todd Rundgren***

Whenever you discuss being a success in the music business, you should realize that there are two distinct areas to consider. One is art and the other is business. The former puts wealth into your heart, and the latter puts money into your pocket. True art is one of the loftiest accomplishments of man, but unfortunately, you can't go to the 7-Eleven and purchase this week's groceries by serenading the store manager with your latest song. That's where the business part comes in. I assume that you're reading this book because you want to be able to earn your living from music. To do that, you have to be serious. This is not a game even though it is full of game players. To take a genuine shot at the pot of gold at the end of this rainbow usually requires at least a couple of years of solid effort.

* © *Rock-Pop 4/24/77*

The first thing you have to do is decide if you really are serious about all this. A lot of people get involved in the music industry and later give it up, wondering what they ever saw in it. As a kid it was fun to pretend to be a cowboy for a couple of hours, but as an adult, the fun burns out rather quickly. Unfortunately, it usually takes us a lot longer to admit we're tired and give up the game.

If you're really serious about succeeding in the music business, you've got to be willing to starve a little, because you're going to be poor before you're going to be rich. Not just poor in dough, but poor in ego and other things as well. You're dealing with a world of opinions that includes club owners who walk up in the middle of your best song and turn the amps off, and friends who tell you that you're wonderful for five years and then ask you why you're wasting your life away on music. Once again, the way through the maze is being aware of reality.

The first cold reality you must face is the one in your checkbook. You have to have a means of support while you're learning your trade (and unfortunately sometimes for a good while after you've mastered it). You're going to have to put in a good deal of effort if you intend to be proficient on an instrument or if you want a career in the business side of music. And there's no guaranteed reimbursement (unless you consider beer and pizza reimbursement. Initial gigs are often at small clubs for free beer, and, if you're lucky, a pizza. Only nowadays you can get thick crust pizza without having to do any more songs).

Being serious is making a commitment to reality rather than fantasy, and sometimes that means a commitment to frustration rather than a nice secure illusion. It's "safer" to believe that the schmuck you met at some party is really as big a deal and as interested in you as he said. The reality probably is that he's just concerned with impressing you, and if he told you he knows someone close to the top at Capitol, it means his sister mops the 10th Floor. A band I worked with in Nashville had an excellent chance of being picked up by another label if they could have faced the reality that things were not happening with their old one. Instead, they pretended everything was hunky-dory until the record got released and their company's distribution department turned out to be a guy with a pickup truck. You just can't approach this business in a storybook fashion. The funny thing is that people with the worst fantasies often think they are taking a cold, realistic view. That includes me and that probably includes you.

Even though you would like to form a band with your two best friends, your brother, and your sister on vocals, it just may not be realistic to do it that way. People who are in the business more as a hobby than a gut-wrenching battle can form bands with their friends and relatives (they can form them with their dogs for all I care). If you want to sell records, however, you have to be concerned with achieving your best because, in all probability, that's what it will take. You must accept the reality that there are a whole lot of people out there trying to do the same thing you are. I look at the music industry as a big fishbowl with a little opening at the top. There are all kinds of wonderfully talented fishes in there, but only room for a few to peek out of the hole where they might be noticed. If you want to be one of them, you've got to learn certain things about business.

## Professional Attitude—Not Advertising That You're An Idiot

Just because a band is fun doesn't give you the right to treat it like it was a toy, *especially* if it sounds like one. The amount of money it takes to properly outfit a band for even small-time gigs is a pretty hefty sum and, unless you're independently wealthy, you can't afford to screw around (incidentally, if you are independently wealthy, you might give me a call . . . I've got some great investments for you). It's also important to remember that time is money, so don't waste a lot of that either. If you keep aware of the commitment you've made, you're more likely to have a professional attitude.

Despite yet another myth, you are in a business which requires you to be businesslike in many situations. By businesslike I don't mean a suit and tie. I used to wear a suit and tie in Nashville and then pick my nose in the guy's office (this did

little to enhance my professional image). By professional attitude, I mean not walking into a club and saying something like,
"We're a new band and we've got to learn somewhere, so how
about letting us make our mistakes in your club?" Talk to a club
owner the same way you would talk to any prospective employer—with tact and respect.

So many folks think that the music business is so hip that
it's cool to cut yourself a little slack. It might be cool to cut yourself a little slack if you're the hottest songwriter, guitar player,
or producer in Hollywood, but in most cases, cutting slack
means you don't eat. It gets to the point where, if you don't
have a professional attitude, anyone who does will shine you on
so fast you'll never know what hit you. If you're always wondering what's wrong, maybe it's because outwardly you look
as if you don't know what's right. You see, in this business most
people *look* as if they have it all together even if they are question marks inside. It's sort of like the lights are on, but nobody's
home.

One of the biggest problems in the music business is the lack
of a business attitude among creative people. Creative people
have to work at business because they usually don't like it. Too
often they wind up playing at it and get eaten alive. Try taking
a "creative approach" to paying your bills and see what I mean.
This is one of the reasons creative people are so susceptible to
being used. Some artists realize this, but instead of learning
how to protect themselves, they just become paranoid (you
know the guy—wants you to sign an agreement before he lets
you hear his tape).

Accept that, businesswise, you're probably a dodo. Then do
something about it. Just because you can keep a balance in your
checkbook doesn't mean that you know how to do business.
And in a business that deals with intangibles like creativity,
art, and feeling, you're even more susceptible to personal
managers, agents, business managers, attorneys, accountants,
and the jackals of the world. So don't take chances. You can
expect to be poor before you get rich and, if you don't learn
about business, you can expect to be poor again after you get
rich. Most people never think about what to do with the money

once it comes in. When my first dough came in, I believed my managers, attorneys, and accountants who were telling me all the wonderful things they were going to do for me. When the dough was all gone and I was screwed and tatooed, they were gone too. They left with the last check.

It doesn't matter that you are not, by nature, good at business. You can still learn enough to keep your shirt by just paying attention. You could check out a book on economics, but that won't help a tenth as much as learning by experience. Just stop tuning out whenever someone talks about business matters. Most artists go into an automatic snooze as soon as they hear words like budget or debit. You can learn a lot about taking care of yourself by letting some sap in a bar tell you how he was screwed out of his shoe store in Peoria. The more you know, the more you are in control, and the less you are at the mercy of others. Start paying attention to human nature as well. Everyone has different abilities and talents, and they also have strengths and weaknesses of character (example: if one of your roadies has been sent up twice for grand theft auto, don't give him a set of keys to the equipment truck). Keep aware of these things and you'll make fewer mistakes.

## Realizing Your Limitations

Don't form a band whose sound is based on four part harmony if none of you can sing. In other words, don't go for something beyond your capabilities. It's important to realize your limitations; that way you can overcome the ones you can, and keep the rest from getting in your way. You also have to be aware of your strengths, and it may be just as difficult to be objective with yourself in that area.

New bands should have an incubation period. If they're inexperienced (and sometimes even if they aren't) they should start out learning other people's tunes (*Hint:* Do not start out trying to master Side Two of Abbey Road). Unless you feel a pull toward a certain direction, work-in as many different types of pop songs as you can, in order to learn a wide variety of styles. Understanding how other people put songs together will enhance your own creativity. As you learn, let your feelings and preferences determine your musical direction. It is during this incubation period that you will discover your talents and enhance your tastes.

You must base your audio goals on the talents you have rather than those you admire. You should do the kind of material that feels best to you. When you perform what you enjoy, it shows in your on-stage personality and even in your sound. Before you set any rigid goals for your band, you must allow your talents to develop enough to lead you in the right direction. How long this takes depends upon how hard you are willing to work. Musicians who have already been down the road with other bands should already know their individual fortés and preferences (by down the road, I mean more than winning the Bird Park Battle of the Bands or something equally trivial). Experienced musicians can do a lot of head-planning on a new band before they even pick up their instruments. They also need to remain flexible however, because the band may take another turn after it gets going.

We're dealing with emotions and sound which are things you can't see. When you hear a tape, you should be able to decide whether you like it or not, but it may not be easy to explain why. Did you ever see the kids on American Bandstand try to explain why they don't like a record ("the beat don't match my feet")? With sound, most people are not technical enough to pick apart a piece of music correctly. Maybe the rhythm is not happening, or the vocalist is slightly off-key, but it just translates to the listener as "crummy." When you don't like something about your music, you'd better stop right there and try to figure it out. And when you figure it out, you'd better do something about it. It may be creative for all the members of the band to play in different time signatures, but does it sound good?

## Kicking Your Brother Out Of The Band

What happens after your 15th audition turns out to be as bad as the previous fourteen? It seems as though all 15 experiences point to one weakness. Your drummer is playing 3/4 time in hard rock tunes. In other words, he stinks. Once you've checked out any criticism according to the guidelines in Chapter One, and it seems consistent, you need to *take action*. If you're good, you should already have an idea of what is wrong. Now all you have to do is face it. If your brother started playing bass by ear six months ago, and he likes throwing his head back and pretending to be Jack Bruce more than he likes to practice, that may be your first clue. If he plays like he's got stubs instead of hands, you know what to do.

Rhythm problems plague most new bands and either the drummer, bass player, or rhythm guitarist should know if something is wrong. How many gigs can you go through where three-quarters of the band is complaining about one member? A band is only as strong as its weakest member, and a solo artist is only as good as his accompaniment. All parts of your engine must be running smoothly if you expect to get anywhere. The weakest link will show like a neon thumb and that is always what the professional people notice first. Unfortunately, they don't look for the high spots nearly as much as they do the weak ones. If one member of a five man band eats it, the other four suffer as well.

If you do have to replace a band member, the best source is from the musicians you know and respect. If none of them provide you with good leads, you will have to go through an outside source. Many cities have organizations which register musicians and for a fee they will turn you on to a number of players that fit your specific needs. One such organization, Professional Musicians Referral (part of Boyd Hunt Enterprises in Minneapolis), is a national referral service which screens and qualifies their listings and has information on over two hundred thousand musicians across the country. Another way to find musicians is to put the word out through advertising. When you advertise for a musician, be as specific as possible about the music, pay, and commitment involved. It's to your advantage to construct an ad that reduces the calls down to only those who are sincerely interested in playing under the conditions you require. One of the biggest drags is setting up a rehearsal and trying out someone who is miles away from your style of music or ability. It is good to shoot a little above your head when looking for a new member, but keep within reason. Don't get carried away and advertise for Eric Clapton at twenty bucks a week, because nobody will respond.

If you're playing on a regular basis and you want to replace your bass player, don't tell him to leave before you've found someone to take his place, or you may have to cancel some gigs. Just set up extra rehearsals; when you've found the right person, give your old bass player a week or two notice, just like any employer would do. Obviously, there is a certain amount of tact necessary to avoid hurt feelings.

When auditioning new players, don't wind up taking somebody on because he has a nice personality. Personality doesn't play bass. On the other hand, be aware of conflicts, because that will only lead to more replacements. Remember, you may have to share a motel room on the road with the new member, and if you can't stand him, it won't matter how good a player he is.

The key is having the right balance in every situation. There will always be a weakest link, but you want to be sure that the rest of the band isn't being held back by one member. When it's time to replace a band member, even if it's your mother (remember the Cowsills?), prolonging the issue usually only makes things worse. Your sound will suffer, your emotions will suffer, and nobody will wind up happy—especially you and the person whose feelings you are trying to protect.

## Making Decisions, Plans, & Goals

You don't have to be an ogre to be successful, but you do have to be realistic enough to make hard decisions which may cause others to be unhappy. Obviously, things can't always work out to please everybody. If the band is doing harmony type tunes, and the harmonies suck wind, realize that it isn't working, and don't make a big deal out of it. Change to easier parts without pondering it for a week or two while nothing gets done. Time is precious unless you want to spend the rest of your life show-casing in your uncle's garage.

You might work for a long time on a particular tune and then perform it at a gig, only to find that it sounds like an out-of-tune garbage disposal. In some cases, you need to have the moxy to admit it doesn't work, rather than to keep working on it and beating a dead horse. You have to be able to make these kinds of decisions because they represent an incredible amount of potentially wasted time. Making decisions quickly will speed the advancement of your career in a big way. Of course, some-times you will make the wrong decisions, but in many cases that is better than making no decision at all.

You need a definite plan, or at least an outline of how you intend to pursue your career. You can't schedule the rate of your act's development; but on the other hand, you just can't wait for things to come together. It's good to have alternate plans. When Plan A fails, move on to Plan B, and when that fails, switch to Plan C (when Plan Z fails, sell your guitar and get a job in a gas station). Set goals within loose time limits, and outline what needs to be done to achieve those goals.

If you miss your goal, just push forward with a new plan. One problem in goal setting is that we tend to despair if we miss our goal. The goal is nothing more than a tool to help move your career along in an organized and progressive fashion. Understand that there will be times when you inadvertently set an unreachable goal. Often we set unrealistic goals because we are unaware of some of the things involved. That's okay—in fact, that is one of the purposes of goal setting. It is better to realize that you were being unrealistic about a certain area of your career than to keep blowing opportunities because of that blind spot.

If your primary goal is becoming a successful recording artist, you should write out a description of what you feel would constitute that success. Be as specific as possible and try to create a visual picture of success in your mind. The importance of having a positive attitude, in this or any other business, can not be overstated. Many of this century's most successful men believe that the best way to attain success is by programming your mind to accept it. Since you've already been conditioned to believe that you will fail in the music business, you need to do something positive to offset the negative.

One good way to develop a positive attitude is to start and end each day by repeating your goal. State it in terms of "I will" rather than "I want." You should also keep phrases like "if I'm lucky" and "in spite of the overwhelming odds" out of your description, because they tend to be demoralizing. The point of writing and repeating your primary goal is to build up your confidence, so don't undermine yourself by letting others dump their doubts on you. You have to be realistic, but you also have to believe in your talent. Above all, don't fall into the trap of feeling sorry for yourself. I know guys who actually enjoy failing so they can talk about how rough things are for them.

Once you have your primary goal set, you need to break it down into four or five secondary goals. If your primary goal is to one day receive a gold record, for example, your first secondary goal would probably be obtaining a recording contract (unless you plan on buying all 500,000 records yourself). Other secondary goals would be obtaining good representation (a manager and/or agent), creating a strong live show, and writing or finding some excellent songs to record. You could have more, but that's enough to keep you busy.

Now you're ready for your working goals, which in some ways are the most important of all. Let's say that you decide the best way to work on your live show is by playing clubs, so your first working goal is learning twenty songs by other artists. Your second working goal might be to write or discover ten original songs. Before you can pursue any other secondary goals, you must master these two working goals.

This is where most artists blow it. They know where they want to go in their career (the dream) and they have some idea about what they should do to get there, but they don't have a daily plan of action based on those goals. Working goals are attainable within a fixed amount of time and they are designed to keep you working. Trying to develop yourself as a recording artist requires you to be your own boss, and that means you have to have some form of discipline. Unless your wife is your manager, there is nobody standing over your bed every morning, telling you to get up and practice your tunes. You've got to *discipline yourself,* and one of the best ways to do it is by having a schedule based upon achieving a working goal. Maybe you figure that, at your best, you could learn seven songs a week and at your very worst you could still handle one a week. Figure an average of three a week and allow seven weeks to learn your twenty songs. If that seems too long, be prepared to learn four songs a week and allow five weeks to achieve your working goal.

You can't schedule more creative functions, like writing, as easily, but that doesn't mean it should be entirely free of discipline. Be more liberal in these areas, but still set a time table and stick to it as best you can. If you miss achieving your working goal you should have learned something about yourself which can help you to be more realistic in your estimate and work habits the next time out. If you never come close to your goals, you're either being too demanding on yourself, or you don't really want to work for your dream. It's up to you to decide which.

After you achieve one working goal, immediately set another. If your time limit runs out, immediately figure a new one. Believe me, goal setting is one of the only ways to keep an artist working effectively toward his dream. And it works even better than chaining him to his piano.

Set your goals along the lines I've described. Break the larger goals down into smaller ones and divide those into working schedules and time-tables. Be realistic and don't rush. Don't plan on going into a four track studio for two hours and cutting Sgt. Peppers. Too many bands try to go from A to Z in one fell swoop. They try to make a record before they can play, and wind up spending most of their time having their egos destroyed by their friendly local A & R men. You don't start with making records. You start with rehearsals, and rehearsals have to be treated like a job. They can be fun, but only if you enjoy working on music.

Use your time. Setting goals will help you remain conscious of this. How many times do you find yourself in a situation where you are idly waiting (waiting for the bus, the doctor, your girlfriend, an agent, the King of Egypt, Miss America, Francis the Talking Mule, etc.)? Use this time constructively by planning ahead for it. In most of these situations you know you will have to wait, so bring along what you need to get some work done. I don't mean setting up your drums in the dentist's office, dummy. I mean doing things like figuring budgets, recopying lyrics, writing out your goals, paying bills, reading, and anything else which requires a minimum amount of material. You'll be amazed at what you can accomplish in the time that you normally spend biting your nails or looking through old National Geographic magazines for pictures of naked native girls. I always carry a leather folder that is full of everything I'm working on because I never know when I will have time to waste. The car breaks down and instead of memorizing the wall map of all the Standard stations in Arizona, I rewrite a scene in my screenplay or correct a chapter of this book.

## The Leader

A band should have a leader. As much as people try it, four guys can't lead a band, because it doesn't work. Bands usually break-up because there's four individuals trying to run things, and differences which began as trivial matters grew into major conflicts. It might be all wonderful at first when everybody is elated with the spirit of democracy in action, but it won't stay that way. The groupies begin telling the singer he's great, and the rest of the band starts to resent him for it. Or the major talent of the group gradually lets his ego get out of hand. There has to be a leader to keep these kinds of situations under control. The leader doesn't have to be the most talented member of the band, but he has to be the smartest business-wise, and he has to have the ability to say yes or no. He should also have some idea of how the music business works (in fact, you should buy him this book). A leader is not necessarily a genius, but he's the guy with the guts to make tough decisions. He's got to be commited and he should be organized and tactful as well.

In every successful unit there's always a leader even if it's not stated as such. You may talk to a band for months and never realize who the real leader is, but that doesn't matter, as long as someone is filling the bill. Sometimes the guys who are the loudest have the least power. The real leader may be very quiet and leading on an unconscious level, but he is still the leader whether the rest of the band realizes it or not.

For your purposes, though, you should have a designated leader. Somebody must make the decisions. Often it doesn't even matter if the decisions are right or wrong, as long as they are decided, because in a learning process like the beginning of a band, there is no real right or wrong. It all helps you grow as long as you learn from the experience and apply it. It's better to make a wrong decision and realize it a month later, than to do nothing for six months except repeat the same old mistakes over and over (repeat some new mistakes over and over for a while). You can't be afraid to take action, and that is a leader's responsibility.

Sometimes you will have a situation where the most charismatic member of the band will think he should be the leader, even though he is the least qualified businessman. If you have a dynamite lead singer on stage who is a pure mellon-head off stage, someone has to make it clear to him that, while he can be the "leader" on-stage, someone else has to call the shots in the real world. The sooner you do this, the better, because there is no getting around the situation. It will eventually rear its ugly head, so head it off at the pass. Establish the responsibilities of the band members from the outset, including who is the leader. Any tenderness of ego should be dealt with at this point.

If you have a "prima-donna" and you can't change him, you must decide how much he is worth to you. Sit down and really have a talk with him about responsibility. Conflict and confrontation are good when done tactfully. If the guy is too lazy, nobody will be able to work with him, but if he is good on stage, he must have put some effort into it, and all you want to do is keep him at that level of commitment. If he won't put out the required effort, you should consider whether his talent is worth the hassle. Maybe you don't mind going over to his place three hours early and dumping ice on his head just to make sure he comes to practice, but the last thing you need is to be a babysitter in your own band. Once again, you have to make the decision.

## Image

When the music starts coming together, it is time to consider the kind of image you want to convey to the public. Would you like to be a Cadillac, Porsche, Datsun, or 1953 Rambler? Image is very important, and worth some thought. Remember that an image is something that is used to sell you to the public and not something by which you must live your life. Many pop stars have made the tragic mistake of subconsciously living out their image. Once Janis Joplin accepted the image of a down-and-out "woman with the blues" she was subconsciously gearing her life around being unhappy. When Jim Morrison continued to live as a psychotic genius off stage, he forfeited his chance to be anything else. People can change, but images have a way of lasting forever. Look at Frank Sinatra, Pat Boone, or Mick Jagger. Don't become or feel a responsibility to your image once you step down from the stage. Alice Cooper is still around as a leading rock star because he recognizes that Alice is a character of his creation and has no life off-stage. Off-stage, Vincent Furnier does not allow himself to be dominated by the macabre Alice. If he did, he would probably be dead.

Choose an image that is compatible with what audiences like about your music. Identify what attracts people to your sound and translate that into visual terms. Is it rebelliousness, slickness, truth, or what? Once you correctly identify this element and its visual translation, it becomes easier to design posters, photos, album covers, and the like (if your audience is middle-aged farmers, don't try to come off like Jimi Hendrix).

It's good to have the image that you want firmly established in your mind before you lock horns with a record company. They might whip an image on you that could prove to be very uncomfortable. Record labels have been known to make mistakes in this area. They don't always care if the image they design suits the act artistically, and sometimes it is a commercial blunder as well. Would you like to be known as a maniac or a sugar baby?

## The Artist as Vendor

In the beginning, an unknown artist has to fulfill all of the various services that are at the disposal of a major artist. You've got to be agents, concert promoters, publicists, road managers, engineers, producers, writers, photographers, managers, attorneys, and your own groupie. If you have any qualms about selling yourself, you're in the wrong business. You can't have the attitude that, because you're an artist, selling and promoting is beneath you (even though it is). You have to promote to get anywhere, and when you're starting out, you have to do it for yourself because no one else will do it for you. Why should an agent spend time trying to book an unknown act when he can book high level talent with much less effort? A top agent can make ten phone calls a day and book ten gigs for a major act at $15,000 each. That's 10% of $150,000, so don't be surprised when he doesn't leap at the chance to book you into Paul's Pizza for fifty bucks a night.

When you're getting together in the garage, you don't need 8 X 10's. When you're trying to get gigs, however, you have to have some promotional material. Because you are your own agent, manager, and publicity person, it's up to you to assemble the right things to promote your act. This means you need to write a promotional letter and have some photos taken (more on this is Chapter 4, *"The Stage & Rehearsal"*).

It's also up to you to contact clubs and book your act. It's better to do this in person, but you should also learn to sell over the phone. Contact the clubs which are on your level of ability (you probably won't sell out the L.A. Forum on your first gig) and ask them if you can have an appointment to play your tape, and leave some promotional material. (We will cover demos in Chapter 5.)

You have to handle getting your equipment to the gig and setting it up, so figure on getting dirty once in a while and learning a bit of electronics. You're also your own sound man, you produce your own demos, write your own contracts, and make your own deals. At times you will probably even organize and promote your own concerts as well. Not only do you need to learn how to do all these things, but you need to learn how to do them on very little money (billboards on Sunset Blvd. are out, at least until you get your first steady gigs).

There's another side to doing all this work yourself. It's good for you because you need to learn how it is done. When it comes time to turn these aspects of your career over to others, you will know how the job should be performed and be able to tell when someone isn't doing it. It may not seem like it at the time, but all these jobs are worth doing for the experience alone.

As you go along, you will meet others you can entrust with some of the responsibility. Every band, for example, has an equipment man who thinks they're the hottest thing since sliced bread. Let him help get the promo out, increase his responsibility as he shows his capabilities, and don't be surprised if one day he becomes your manager. But it is also very important not to involve too many people too quickly. You have to keep control of what is happening at all times, and group mentality can really reduce awareness. Surround yourself with too many yes-folks, and pretty soon you think the sun rises and sets at the tip of your nose.

A new artist has to have eyes in the back of his head. You are competing with many others for the attention and time of those who can help your career. There are a lot more artists who desire a career in music than there are qualified people who can help them. On the other hand, don't make the mistake of thinking you're competing with the band across the street. Too often, unknown acts refuse to help each other because of a sense of competition. Artists can really assist each other with things like equipment, transportation, and knowledge, and everybody needs all the help he can get. So don't let ego get in the way, and make friends instead of enemies. The truth is that you are more in competition with Led Zeppelin than you are with Charley's band across the street. If you're going to compete with someone, compete with someone who is selling two million records, because they are the people who are getting the attention you so desperately need. In short, be aware, but don't compete.

You can sound great, but if your business presentation is so bad that nobody will listen to you, it won't do you any good. The Beatles had great tunes, but they were too unprofessional to get a listen until Brian Epstein cleaned them up and started making the rounds (they used to scream English obscenities at uncomprehending German audiences).

You promote yourself in everything that you do. The way you look, talk, dress, walk, and act are all advertisements for yourself. For a new artist, it is as important to look competent in business meetings as it is to be exciting on stage. You're not going to get an A & R person (Artist & Repertoire, or Antagonism & Rejection) to come down to the local C.Y.O. and hear your band if you act like an idiot in his office.

## What Labels Look For

As mentioned in Chapter 1, record companies are interested in something that is unique and professional. The band has to be tight and the vocals have to be great. If the vocals aren't there, you can forget it. Arif Mardin, of Atlantic Records, says flatly, "The vocal sound is the most important thing on a demo."* So unless you're planning on being the next Crusaders (instrumental only), you had better have a good singer. Instruments can't talk, and the first thing the listener goes for is the lyrics and the sound of that singer's voice. If that's not happening, most people will tune out right there. They may not understand the lyrics, but they have to like the sound of the voice, or they won't keep listening.

Labels also look for a group that is together off stage as well as on. You'd be surprised at how much good character is a factor. Nobody wants to sign someone who might be in jail or dead from an overdose a week later.

Solid representation is *very* important. In fact, most labels

* © *Chicago Daily News* (*"Producers: The Studio Stars" by James Riordan 1/26/78*).

won't touch an act unless they've got good management and an agent. If you hit L.A. from Omaha and you're really, really good, but all you've got is a small-time agent and no manager, the labels won't be too thrilled. Record companies realize that most artists are stupid businessmen. Actually, they think *all* artists have no business sense and that talking business to an artist is a waste of time. They just want to talk to the artist about his music. When it comes time to talk about business and departing with their hard-earned dollars, they want to talk to someone with a business mind. Naturally, they don't want to turn money over to someone who they don't think can handle it. It's hard enough to get them to turn it over to a manager with a good track record, who they know can get the job done (more about this in a later chapter).

The labels are also going to want to see you perform live, and if you don't knock them out from the stage, they won't be interested in going any further. The record companies know that you are the best salesman your record has got, and that you can sell a lot of records from live appearances. If you're not out there showing off your wares on stage, it will make their job a lot tougher.

Labels also love originality and they especially like an original hit song. It's important for the artist to either write his own songs, or have a writer who works with him. This is something that you should begin developing from the start.

These areas will be discussed throughout the book, but for now, you should be aware of them as you begin to form your sound. You don't want to gear everything to please a label, but if your goal is making records, you should at least know that good vocals, solid representation, character, strong live performance, originality, and a hit song should be part of your plan for success.

# Chapter 3
# The Stage and Rehearsal

*"The stage is like shaping a sculpture and making it work
with the audience. It evolves . . . especially at the beginning of the tour. It takes a certain amount of time to
figure out what's going to work the best."*

**—Lindsey Buckingham,
Fleetwood Mac\***

## Importance of Rehearsal

**Rehearsal is a job.** It is the part that nobody likes, but it is
the key to all the rest. The fruits of rehearsal are exhibited on
stage and in the recording studio, but the work itself often
occurs in garages and basements. The attitude with which you
approach rehearsal will reflect on your entire career. If you are
serious about your career, you had better learn to be serious
in rehearsal.

It is important to leave your nonmusical problems outside the
rehearsal hall. While rehearsing, you have to focus your attention on the job at hand. Bands should set aside some time each

*\* © Rock-Pop 2/17/80*

week to discuss anything of a non-musical nature that relates to the group. If everyone knows that there will be time allowed to hear their gripes, they should be able to relax and devote their energy to the music throughout the week.

When you were first learning your instrument, you had to practice regularly if you were to make any improvement. After your fingers stopped hurting, it became obvious that the more seriously you practiced, the better you became. The same is true for a band in rehearsal, even though the difference may not be obvious on a daily basis. Bands tend to make jumps from one musical plateau to another, rather than slow, steady progress, but the better you rehearse, the less time between jumps.

## How To Rehearse

**Don't waste time.** Some bands rehearse five nights a week for five hours each night and get about as much done as they could in two evenings of real effort. Utilize your time in rehearsal. How many bands have you known whose rehearsal pattern goes something like this: Practice is set to start at 7:00 p.m., so the guitar player is the first to arrive at 7:15. Rehearsals are held at the keyboard player's house and when the drummer arrives at 7:30, all three members start setting up their equipment. They have to set up every weekend so that the keyboard player can work on his boat between rehearsals. When the singer arrives at 8, he is uptight because nobody knows where the bass player is. Since the bass player has no phone, the singer leaves to go to his house in case he is sleeping again. The equipment is set up by 8:15, when the bass player arrives. Since the singer is still gone, the drummer decides to grab a burger at McDonald's. When the drummer returns twenty minutes later, the singer and the bass player are arguing and the keyboard player is having a philosophical discussion with the guitarist. By ten minutes to nine, everybody is downstairs except the keyboard player, who had to go to the store for his wife. When he returns they decide to "loosen up" with a twenty minute jam. After they take a joint break and work for half an hour on a new song, it's time to quit. They have to stop at ten or the neighbors go crazy. Six months later when they break up, each one of them feels cheated because they "put so much work into the band."

Obviously there are organizational problems that have to be solved for rehearsals to progress smoothly. You have to have a place where you can leave your equipment set up, so work towards that goal right away. Everyone must be on time and you have to get started as soon as possible. Loosening up is okay, but don't jam all night. Try to get at least three hours of solid work in every time you rehearse.

The reason rehearsals become such a drudge is that all members are not thinking and working as a unit. They often get off the track as to why they are there. They seem to forget that they are not getting a paycheck at the end of the week for rehearsing, so they treat it as if they were punching a clock. Remember, you are rehearsing because of your own choosing, and the time you are wasting is time that you could spend in a much more enjoyable way. There is a definite amount of work to be done and you don't get paid a cent until you do it.

Some people have the attitude that anything not done in a formalized job situation is meant to be a party. If you are using rehearsals as an excuse to party, you will make this business twice as tough as it needs to be. Remember that every hour you spend screwing around in rehearsal is time taken away from writing or polishing your individual chops. On the other hand, you don't have to treat rehearsals like they are the coal mines of Pennsylvania either. You can get a lot done and enjoy yourself at the same time. You must enjoy working on music or you wouldn't be pursuing it. Too many bands have the attitude that rehearsals are a drag by nature, so the best thing to do is to party with the hope of making it as enjoyable as possible. Wrong.

**Rehearsals should be structured** so that the greatest amount of work can be accomplished in the least amount of time. The leader should have planned out what to work on at rehearsal. Any "homework" should be assigned and agreed upon by the individual involved (just because the bass player is the only member of the band who has a copy of Sgt. Peppers', doesn't mean that you should expect him to figure out all the chords to the songs before Saturday's practice).

You can't say exactly how many tunes you will be able to learn in one rehearsal, but you can know the order in which you should work. Working out one tune to the point where everyone agrees on the arrangement and is satisfied with his performance is a hell of an accomplishment. Taping rehearsals can speed up the process and provide you with a source of objectivity.

Sometimes rehearsals are a drag because of a weak link problem. Everyone is burned out on going through the tune an extra twenty times for the bass player. Everyone will have problems on different songs, but if one member is having problems on every song, you know what must be done.

**Rehearsals should be closed.** If the wives and kids have to come, make them stay in another room. You don't want a lot of people around, because there are already enough different individuals to handle within the context of the band. Rehearsals are not the place for girlfriends, wives, or "friends of the band." Everybody sits there and claps and hoots. It really enforces the party atmosphere. You wind up doing stupid things like performing the songs you know best (and need to work on the least) so that your friends can hear how good the band is coming along. Rehearsals are the last place to show off. Everybody must be able to let their hair down at rehearsal, and one extra person can keep that from happening.

Another good reason to keep people away from your rehearsals is to prevent you from having to deal with their opinions. Whether it's the drummer's wife or the singer's best friend, their opinion carries some weight with that member and it can affect your band. Just because the drummer's sixteen year old wife (who has almost no concept of how music is made) thinks the band isn't coming together fast enough, she can put a lot of pressure on him. And when it comes time for everyone to sign for an equipment loan, guess who can't do it unless he wants a divorce? Believe me, it's much easier if you just tell everyone they can check out the band at a gig when you're ready and able to put on a good performance.

## The Stage

The first major objective of a new band should be to perfect their live performance. The stage is where you can show off your expertise to your friends and the rest of the world. More importantly, it is where you truly learn what being a performer is all about.

To get gigs, you need to have a good representation of your act on tape. If you are going to be playing the Top 40 bars, include the more popular songs that you perform well. This "club demo" should be good quality, but no better than a four track. Don't overdub or else the club owners will question your ability to perform the songs live. Five or six songs should be enough to give them a good idea, and if you can obtain a good quality tape of a live performance, that would be the route to go. In addition, you need a press kit complete with pictures, a bio, and a list of credits and references. The more clubs you have played, the easier it is to get jobs.

If you want to concentrate full time on this stage of your career, you should get a little league agent. A little league agent books bars and high school dances. They are usually located in large cities and handle acts with names like "The Margueritas," "Three Guys & A Girl," and "The In Crowd." Little league agents have a tendency to paste up pictures of all their acts on their office walls and act more important than they really are, but the good ones can help your career immensely. Don't sign an exclusive contract with them for longer than a year, however, because you want to keep moving upwards. Most of these agents are under the opinion that it is impossible to make it in the big time, and they will try to discourage you as much as they can. It is better not to tell them that you are just playing bars to develop your stage act before going on to original songs. They may not book you if they think that you won't be a career bar band.

Decent bar bands can earn over two grand a week, which makes for a pretty nice living, considering you're in apprenticeship. One more thing that is absolutely essential to get gigs is a professional attitude. Reread this section in Chapter 2 before you begin hustling gigs.

## The Stage And Records

A working artist is the only kind of artist who interests most record companies. You really shouldn't begin considering your recording possibilities until your act is together and you are going over well with audiences. To do so before is putting the cart before the horse. If, by some miracle, you were able to get a record deal before mastering the stage, you will die a quick death once you hit the road. If you've got a hit record and don't come off superprofessional in concert, they will laugh you off the stage. And then you've got one hit worth of royalties, a blown ego, and a screwed up career.

Once you are consistently blowing the audiences away and you've mastered on-stage rapport on both good and bad nights, it is time to consider a recording career. To do so before may be a waste of time, but to fail to make the jump to recording when you're ready can be equally disastrous (more about that later).

If you are already recording an album, you should realize that the stage is the best place to sell it. Every successful concert sells an incredible amount of product. Despite the fact that this is a business of hype, a concert only succeeds if the crowd likes the act, and if they do, they will respond by buying the artist's record. Let's say you're a member of Rick & The Rags, on your first tour of medium size clubs throughout the country. Your album is out and it's obvious that it isn't a smash. It's now up to you to create excitement for it through your concerts.

The average crowd at these gigs is three hundred folks, but the label is supporting you with local radio spots, and some of the stations in each area are playing your single. If you can blow the audience away every night, you can turn your album into a good seller. Even if only 25 people buy it after seeing you in concert, you can bet that they will play it for another hundred. The impression you made with one concert may wind up getting you strong local airplay and three hundred loyal fans. There's something special about seeing an act before they hit. From that point on, the audience at those early concerts will regard you as a "hometown" act because they saw you before you were big. If you can have that kind of effect in fifty different cities, your career is made. The local record stores start telling the promo men, and they tell the label. The label puts out more hype. All of a sudden you're getting airplay all over the country and the major market stations pick up on it. On the strength of major airplay, you back-up a heavy act in front of ten thousand people. You knock 'em dead because you've got your stage show very together. Pretty soon you're the supporting act on a major tour and your album is selling like crazy. All because you thoroughly mastered the stage before you put your ass on the line.

## Mastering The Stage

There is no stage without an audience. The crowd is your purpose for being there. When you're on stage, you are trying to get people to appreciate your music. You want them to feel justified for paying to see you and be eager to see you again. The first step in being good on stage is getting your act as musically tight as possible. You want to have every song you perform down perfectly. The arrangements should be the way you want them and you should be happy with your performance of them. This work is all done in rehearsal.

The next step in conquering the stage can be practiced in rehearsal, but only perfected on the stage itself. You must develop a show. When you're on stage, you don't just stand there and play your songs (unless you're Pink Floyd and can afford to have a megadollar light and film show going on behind you). You're an entertainer, so learn to be entertaining. Move around and put as much feeling into your playing as you can without going into orbit. In fact, go ahead and go into orbit as long as you don't blow any notes.

Hopefully, you will be able to create a good show by just letting go and releasing your energy. Sometimes this will be all you need to do. Some bands are so in synch that they just naturally look great on stage. Others look awkward and the individuals members work against each other. It's good to have an objective observer (your manager perhaps) help you perfect your stage show. The ideal is to video tape yourself and work it out that way, but that may be too expensive. Looking good on stage takes time and experience to achieve, but it is something that you should always be working toward. (Donnie & The

Deadbeats with their half-asleep, half-hypnotised approach to the stage went out of style after too many of their audiences died from boredom). If you just want to stand there, don't bother playing "live." If you can't add to your record by putting in a little action, playing gigs will only hurt your sales. Just have the record company send life size cardboard cut-outs and recorded music to your concerts instead.

After you have perfected your music and developed a kick ass show, there is still one more important step to mastering the stage. You must learn to recognize and play to your audience. I don't mean telling Henny Youngman jokes or juggling anchovies. I mean gauging an audience and doing what you know appeals to them. In the beginning you will face many different kinds of audiences and you will either learn how to play an audience, or suffer through some of the worst experiences of your life. Once your sound is well known, you will draw a crowd that already likes you, and this will be less of a problem. But what you learn about controlling an audience in the early stages of your career can make you an absolute show stopper in the years to come.

The best way to learn how to please an audience is by not giving up when you've got a hard one. When you're starting out, some of the crowds you will get will be absolutely awful. They'll hate you on sight. Everybody gets bad gigs, but you can turn them into learning experiences. Really horrible gigs usually come from going into a place blind without knowing what kind of an audience you will draw. Say you find yourself in a rowdy hill-billy club in south Louisiana and you're an all black soul band from Detroit. Or maybe you're into anti-war acid rock, and you find yourself on a tour of military bases. It can get tense. Some friends of mine were in a group that did a lot of very avant-garde music and sarcastic comedy. They went over very well at colleges and anywhere that offered them an intellectual audience. Their agent booked them into this bar in Georgia and when they got there, they found that it was a very red-neck sort of place. The stage was a kind of loft which was enclosed in chicken wire. The manager told them that once the stairway door was locked, the only way up there would be a ladder that they were to take up with them. He explained the chicken wire and the ladder by saying, "The crowd gets kind of rowdy here." They thought he was kidding. Roughly a hundred beer bottles were bounced off the chicken wire screen that night and the ladder was not lowered until two hours after the club had closed. Needless to say, their option was not picked up.

Check out your audiences and the way they respond to certain elements in your act. How old are they, what sex are they, how rowdy are they, and what are their musical tastes? Are they just out to have a good time or do they expect to be enlightened as well? Learn what they like and learn to *deliver* it. You are there to do a job and that job is pleasing the audience. If you are only interested in pleasing yourself on stage, don't bother going on. Instead, showcase in your living room in front of the big mirror.

Don't fall into the trap of judging your audience. Analyze them, but don't judge them. Blaming a bad gig on the crowd is not even okay when it's true. Don't let yourself feel depressed because you didn't go over with an audience that you had no business even performing for, but at the same time try to learn from the experience. Blaming it on the audience will lead to giving up when you have a difficult crowd. When faced with an audience of deaf mass murderers or one-armed Russian immigrants, don't expect a lot of applause, but don't quit trying to win them over. As a performer, you have to remain loose and viable and willing to change with your audience.

Obviously, I don't mean trying to pull off "Foggy Mountain Breakdown" if you're a jazz band. Don't adapt to the point where you lose your sincerity. The most important thing you can convey to an audience is that you are sincere about what you are doing. The next most important thing to communicate is that you enjoy what you do and you want them to enjoy it too. If you can deliver on all three of those points, you're home free.

## The Stage As A Testing Ground

While you shouldn't feel bad about learning Top 40 material in order to please the audience in the bar clubs, there comes a time when you must move into more original music. You can perfect your band, your show, and improve the way you handle an audience by playing bars, but to be a successful recording artist, you must be able to perform new material as well. If you don't write, you need to look for someone who does; but until you find such original material, you can start arranging other songs into a style of your own. It is also good to pick out a few obscure album cuts that are not well known and see what you can do with them.

Adding more originality to your act will probably necessitate moving into clubs that are geared more to the concert performance than dancing. This may cause you some fear, and a financial setback, but remember you are not doing this to play clubs the rest of your life. Learning how to win over an audience by playing Beach Boy songs is fine, but now it's time to move on to something else. Once you have your stage act together, the more original material you learn, the closer you are to getting a record deal and playing the big time. So jump right in.

The stage is a great place to test out new material and arrangements. Look at it as a proving ground. It is the best place to find out which of your tunes have the effect that you are looking for on an audience. It's true that some songs are better suited to be heard on a phonograph than in a live performance, but that is also something you can learn better by doing. Learn how to develop and deliver your songs with power and sincerity, and watch the audience's reaction. This is how you narrow down the field for your demo.

Once you have consistently blown audiences away by performing original tunes or arrangements, it is time to embark on a recording career. Understand that you are entering a new world. The lessons you've already learned have prepared you, but there are new lessons awaiting you. You're not going to become a major star playing every beer bar in America. You need records to reach the masses, so now it's time to learn how to make them.

# Chapter 4
# The Song

*"The songs have got to relate to people. The purpose of many of my songs is to shorten the distances between people so they're not so alone. The words have got to mean something. They have to . . . otherwise there is no reason to have them."*

**—Graham Nash** *

The song is the key to the ballgame. It unlocks all the doors to the yellow brick road. You can't say enough about how important it is to the success of a record. You can have a cooking band, a great producer, and a tremendous marketing campaign, but without the right song, none of it is worth a broken guitar string. You can be Tommy & The Ten Pins fresh out of the local bowling alley, have your dog for a producer, and a marketing campaign financed by your school lunch money, and with the right song, it could work.

There are songs and then there are *hit* songs. While you can't teach someone how to write a hit, the aim of this chapter is to

* © *Rock-Pop 10/23/75*

familiarize you with the elements involved in writing and marketing such songs. Hopefully, this will prick your own creative desires.

## Writing Songs

More than any other kind of writing, songs are created rather than crafted. You don't usually sit down to write a song by first drafting an outline and some notes and then proceeding in an orderly fashion. Then again, you *could* do it that way. You could do it any way, and there is no singularly right or best method. Don't try to write songs in a rigid pattern. Songs have to flow. They start in all kinds of ways and develop in every pattern imaginable. There are so many formulas to writing songs that there are no formulas.

As a songwriter, you should never limit yourself to one method, and this is especially true when you're starting out. You might begin a song with the last thing your girlfriend said to you before she slammed the car door on your hand, or you might start with a drum beat that you can't get out of your head. It doesn't make any difference. The trick is to find your own ways of developing those things into full fledged songs.

Don't be hindered in your efforts to write by your own displeasure with your work. Almost everybody starts out writing love songs with words like "thud" and "mud" in them, but keep at it. Don't throw sheets of poetry away because it embarrasses you. Study it and learn what it is that you don't like about it. When you were sixteen you didn't hide your car away in the garage the first time you shifted into the wrong gear, did you? Rewrite your songs until you like them, or until you write something new that you like better. This is true for both music and lyrics. Despite the myth surrounding creativity, you can learn to develop it.

Individual songs may also come in pieces. More often than not, you will come up with a part that you really like, which doesn't fit well with anything you have already written. It may be lyrics without music, or music without lyrics. Paul McCartney once told how he was walking down the street and the melody for "Yesterday" came into his head. He used to sing it using the words "ham and eggs" for the part that later became "Yesterday." He had the melodic hook, but the words didn't come until later.

## Lyrics & Melody

Songs are made up of the words or lyrics, and the melody, or the music. The word "melody" describes the part that is sung, not the music that is played to accompany the singer. The chords and melodies played as accompaniment can be considered an arrangement, but only the vocal melody line is copyrightable as part of the song.

There's a certain knack in writing lyrics which comes with practice and patience. There are particular ways of saying things and forms of rhyme which are essential to songwriting, even though they are somewhat indescribable. You have to be conscious of rhythm. Listen to the songs you like and analyze how the words are structured. Practice writing in various structures. After a while it becomes natural to say things in short bursts of poetry. Lyrics, after all, are poetry with consistent rhythm.

## Hooks

Hit songs usually have a melodic line that is very catchy and infectious. It may have lyrics that are the focal point of the song. This part usually repeats throughout the tune and it is the part most people remember when they think of the song. This is the hook, and hit songs are built on good hooks. There are instrumental and rhythm hooks as well as vocal ones. Remember Gerry Rafferty's "Baker Street" with its great saxophone hook?

The vocal hook is usually in the chorus. It's the whole message of the song wrapped up in a few lines. It's the thing that you wake up in the morning singing. It's what pops into your head after you've only heard the song a few times. It's what sells the song.

A lot of good writers start out with the hook. The meat of the tune is usually what comes to the professional songwriter first, but that takes time to develop. After you have been writing a while, you may wake up in the middle of the night and start looking for your cassette player to record the incredible hook line that just came to you in your sleep. Once you've got the germ of the song, you can build on it later. Many writers try to have the hook be the title of their song. Burt Bacharach and Hal David often do this, but they take it one step further. Many of their songs *begin* with the hook line and title, such as "Raindrops Keep Falling On My Head," "The Look Of Love," "What The World Needs Now Is Love," "This Guy," and many others.

Both the lyrics and melody must be right for a song to work. If you have great lyrics but a crummy melody, no one is going to listen. The human ear goes for the lyrics first, but the melody is what enhances them and directs the mind to keep on listening. On the other hand, if a great melody was all it took to have a hit song, Mozart and Bach would be on the Top 40. Obviously it takes both a lyrical and a melodic talent to write hit songs, but don't despair if you are lacking in one of these areas. There are many great songwriters who can not play a lick of music, and others who can't put a single word to their melodies. If you would like to be a songwriter despite a gaping lack of talent in either words or music, pay close attention to this next section.

## Collaboration

Don't limit yourself by your weaknesses. If you're a great poet, don't force your melodies to fit in with the few chords that you can play on the guitar. If you don't think your melodies are doing your lyrics justice, find someone to write with. By the same token, if you write pop symphonies of melody, but your lyrics sound like first grade poetry, you should also start looking for a collaborator. Once again you are required to make a realistic appraisal of your ability and take the necessary action. A lot of writers are too proud to write with someone else, and as a result they are leaping into anonymity faster than the Beatles leaped out.

Collaboration is one of the best ways to write songs. A lot of the people who say they can't write as a team are just afraid to try. You'd be surprised at how easily things fall together when you have the write partner (I'm sorry, I couldn't resist the pun).

There have been several great songwriting teams, and the greatest of our era is Lennon and McCartney. Besides being the most successful recording artists in history, the Beatles were responsible for some of our best songs. The strength of the group was the hit songwriting of Lennon and McCartney which, as I indicated earlier, can make the difference between success and failure. While both men wrote songs by themselves (which they still listed as a team effort), in many cases Lennon supplied the words to McCartney's melodies. This became painfully evident when the Beatles broke up and both Lennon and McCartney released solo albums. McCartney writes beautiful melodies, but usually has very little to say. Lennon writes profound lyrics, but his melodies fail to enhance them. As a team they were the best, but as individuals, their weaknesses are all too obvious.

In team writing there is also the influence that one writer has upon the other's talents. McCartney's lyrical efforts were better when he was with the Beatles because he was influenced by Lennon's poetic abilities. At the same time, Lennon may have taken more care with his melodies because of his awareness of McCartney's talent in that area.

There are many ways of writing as a team. Some collaborators blend their lyrical and melodic abilities rather than specialize in one area or the other. Sometimes they only join forces when one of them gets stuck, or one may write choruses while the other concentrates on verses. There are as many possibilities as there are creative personalities and talents. Many great songs have been combined from two separate songs. Perhaps each collaborator has a song that he isn't happy with, and when the two are joined together, a special sort of magic happens. The most obvious example of this is "A Day In The Life."* McCartney's middle piece ("woke up, got out of bed" etc.)

* © Maclen Music Inc., BMI

blended beautifully and completed the meaning of Lennon's song ("I read the news today, oh boy" etc). Most combination songs are not as different in rhythm as the two that formed "A Day In The Life," but the important thing is that they enhance each other.

Collaborators also inspire each other, which may be more important than their specific talents. The whole is greater than the sum of its parts, or some sort of mathematical garbage like that. Sometimes one collaborator actually writes the song while the other supplies the inspiration, and it is still a team effort. An example of this would be a singer who has good melodic ideas and lyrics, but needs to work with a guitar player in order to focus his abilities. The guitarist might run through some chord changes over and over while the singer does the rest, but it still takes two to make it happen.

There are as many successful song writing teams as there are successful individual writers. It takes excellent musical ability, a flare for melody, arrangement capabilities, and a talent for writing rhythmic poetry to be a good songwriter. So don't throw those lyrics into the trash just because all your melodies sound like "Mary Had A Little Lamb." Six months from now you might run into somebody who has the perfect melody to turn those lyrics into a song, which could turn out to be a great song and win you a Grammy. And you pitched it into the garbage. How callous can you get?

There are uncountable ways to write, and the responsbility of the new writer is to discover his strengths, weaknesses, and the method that works best for him. Don't get trapped into one method or style of writing until you've really allowed yourself to experiment. Some writers are so psyched out that they can only write on one particular piano in one particular room of one particular house. That's being a little too particular, don't you think? If the room collapsed, their songwriting output would collapse with it. On the other hand some guys can write lyrics in the middle of a noisy restaurant with no problem.

Be flexible in the writing process as well. You don't have to start with the beginning of a song. You can start at the end if you want to, or you can start in different places every time you write. Go with the flow. Do what seems best for each particular song. The more rules and conditions you put on your writing, the more you will stifle your natural creative flow, and the flow is the real key to all creativity. Don't *try* to write a hit. Let it flow and then tune in an direct it according to what you have learned. I recommend collaboration because it really helps to overcome the blocks. If one partner starts to lose it, the other can pick it up. Collaboration improves the tools at your disposal and partners can keep each other psyched about the song.

## Being A Songwriter

In terms of creativity and financial gain, songwriting is the most rewarding career in the music business. If you write songs, you probably enjoy it. There is no denying that it is one of the ultimate creative experiences. The people who do it well get so high from the experience that it is more like a hobby than a job to them. If you have the talent, you really ought to pursue it because it involves less expense and less actual time to develop than any other aspect of music. For the cost of taping a song on a little cassette player, or renting a four track, you can literally get a return of millions. Sure, you've got to have the right contacts to get your songs heard, but you have to have that in every career in the music business.

Successful songwriters make incredible amounts of money. I know of several people who have made a million dollars off of one song. Unfortunately, I know more people who have not made one dollar off of a hundred songs. When you think about it, the hit song generates the billing that allows the entire music business to function. More than anything else, it is the song that sells records, so the writer deserves to make considerable money off of a hit. He may write for ten years with no financial reward whatsoever, but one hit can pay for it all.

The bulk of a writer's income is from two sources. They are paid royalties by the record companies, based on the sales of the recordings of their songs. These are called "mechanicals," and they are tabulated at the rate of 2.75 cents per song. It you had three songs on Wynn McFish's new album, and it sells 300,000 copies (a good seller, but not a smash), you would make about $8,250 on each cut, or approximately $24,750 in all from mechanical royalties.

The second way that a songwriter is paid is based on airplay. Every time a song is played on radio, television, or in a major concert, the writer is paid a royalty. As you can imagine, this is a hell of an accounting job. The companies that do it are called licensing agencies, and the established ones are ASCAP, BMI, and SESAC. These companies monitor a representative amount of radio, television, and concerts, and compute how often a particular song is getting played. Airplay royalties vary from a few cents for play on a minor market radio station, to more than $400 for network television. The total often more than doubles the income from mechanicals. The amount of airplay on a major hit record continues on a decreasing basis for a number of years. Those "blasts from the past" that you keep hearing on your local station may still be supporting their writer in fine style.

In addition, songwriters are paid royalties for sheet music sales. This does not compare with the other sources of income, but on a major hit it can be very substantial. Often songs are "leased" to be used in commercials or films and this too can be very profitable.

The more times that a song is recorded, the more money the writer makes. When Vinnie The Fang has a big hit with your song, his money stops with his record sales, but you can earn a pile more from "cover" versions of the song by other artists. Middle-of-the-road tunes are recorded more often than other types of music because there are a whole bunch of artists in that style whose fans want to hear how they sing the latest hits. If, in addition to Vinnie The Fang, your tune is also recorded by Andy Williams, Wayne Newton, Johnny Mathis, and Tony Bennett, you will be eagerly checking your mailbox for years to come. Some songs become what are called "standards," in that they are recorded by several artists every year. "Yesterday," for example, has been recorded over 200 times!

Now that you've heard the good side, let me point out some of the less appealing aspects of being a songwriter. The most difficult thing to accept as a songwriter is that your talent is worth nothing until it's perfected. Poor musicians can play in crummy clubs. In fact, without poor musicians, crummy clubs would be out of business. But a songwriter without a hit is more unwanted than Lawrence Welk at a punk rock concert. You *can't* earn a living as a songwriter unless your songs are being recorded. There is a middle ground, but the chances are that you will either live very comfortably or starve if you depend solely on your songwriting as a means of support. It can be very frustrating, knowing that you're the next Jimmy Webb and having to pump gas instead of push your songs, but you do have to eat. The situation is made more unbearable by having to deal with a lot of fruitcakes who consider themselves publishers, producers, or even artists.

The chances are that you won't be able to get your songs to any reputable producers and artists until you get a publisher. That doesn't mean you shouldn't occasionally give it a shot, but don't waste a whole lot of time on that avenue. Instead, waste time trying to sort out who is a reputable publisher and who is an idiot. For some ungodly reason there are a lot of people screening songs for publishing companies who have no business being there. Some of them are designed to turn away writers and others are not, but the result is the same. It can drive you nuts.

A lot of publishers employ ex-songwriters to listen to new material. While I'm sure this is based on the theory that someone who has written a good song will recognize one, there are a few things wrong with the practice. For one thing, there is no such thing as an ex-songwriter. These guys are all still cranking out the tunes, and the problem is that they are more interested in writing a hit than in discovering one. I will tell you another true story to illustrate my point. Again, the names have been changed to protect the innocent (me). Shortly after I arrived in Nashville, my collaborator and I went to see a well known publishing company. The guy who listened to our tape had co-written a couple of very famous songs a number of years before. Apparently it was too long ago, or else he wouldn't have been sitting at a desk when he would rather have been at a piano.

After he listened to our tape, he asked us if we would like to hear some of his new stuff. Sure, why not? Before I could say "Music City U.S.A.," he brought in a friend from the hall to sing back-up. So the two of them are singing this song *a capella* and you can tell they really, really hope that my friend and I like it. And there we are, wondering why this guy wants to impress two kids who are living in a 1965 Chevy?

## Publishers

A hard working, well connected publisher is the answer to a songwriter's prayer. He can take those rough sparks of genius that you've crudely taped on a General Electric cassette recorder, and turn them into a polished demo that shows off your song to the max. And he can turn that demo into big money in an amazingly short amount of time. That is the ideal. You are looking for a hustler that can't wait to play your songs for the next artist he can get to, and you don't want him unless he can get to as many big names as you can write songs for.

A good publisher will also be able to give you constructive advice on honing your edge as a songwriter. He is a listener, but he understands what he hears. He is a businessman, but he recognizes the needs of creativity. If you don't trust him, or have confidence in his ability to do the job, you are better off not wasting time with him. There are hundreds of publishers out there, so you had better learn to separate the talents from the idiots as fast as you can. This involves knocking on a lot of doors and listening to a lot of bad advice while you look for the right one. It's important to remember that you are checking out these guys as much as they are checking you out. It helps you feel less like a begger who is selling songs instead of pencils.

Unfortunately, not everyone who calls himself a publisher can recognize a great song in demo form, so you have to learn not to be discouraged by opinions. Whenever someone laughs at your love songs, it is good to re-read the *Golden Reel-To-Reel & Platinum Turntable Myth* section in Chapter 1. While you always want to be receptive to constructive advice, there are a lot of publishers whose ears seem to be plugged with the wax of old hit records. All they can hear is what *used* to be happening.

When you see a publisher, take him your four best tunes (with a lyric sheet), recorded as clearly as you possibly can. You don't have to go into the studio, but don't try to get away with using those "eight-for-a-dollar" cassettes either. In general, they should be positive up-tempo songs that anyone could sing. Try to write for the general public according to the songs that you know are popular. Don't be too avant-garde, but don't *try* to be commercial either. Write something you like, that you feel others will like as well. Contact only reputable publishers. If you don't know who they are, get their names from the backs of record albums, or brouse through some sheet music. If you move to one of the music business centers, the best thing to do is to contact ASCAP or BMI and ask their advice. They would be unable to direct you over the phone, but if you visit them, sometimes they can give you some valuable guidance when it comes to finding a publisher.

While most publishing companies claim to listen to tapes they receive in the mail, there is really no way to be sure your song is heard unless it is played in front of you. The amount of contacting you have to do to get a good publisher makes it almost impossible to accomplish by mail. My advice to writers is the same as my advice to recording artists in this area. *When you're ready, head for the city.* If you simply can't move for a while, give the mails a shot, but make some preliminary phone calls first to find out if they are listening to any new material. You might get lucky. In this business, crazy things happen every day.

### Dealing With Publishers

When you sign with a publisher, you are usually giving them the exclusive right to publish all of the songs you write during the period of the contract. You may be required to give them so many new songs a year. They, in turn, agree to record adequate demos and promote those demos to recording artists. The contracts are usually structured so that you receive a fixed royalty rate for sheet music sales, and split your mechanicals (royalties from record sales) with the publisher. So if jazz artist Skitch Skeezix got a gold album (sales of 500,000) and one of your tunes was on it, at the 2.75 statuatory rate, your publisher would get royalty checks from Skitch's label totaling $13,750. Your publisher would then issue you a check for half that amount. The publisher also makes an equal amount of airplay royalties but both he and the songwriter are issued checks directly from the licensing companies.

When you sign an exclusive deal with a publisher, he is representing your catalogue of songs. When you have a hit, that catalogue becomes very valuable because name artists will seek out your material. Consequently, if your publisher believes in you, he should be willing to give you some sort of an advance when you sign the contract. This could take the form of a weekly draw which is equivalent to a normal job salary, or just a lump sum advance.

Your publisher can also negotiate an advance from the licensing companies. Since the license for a publishing company must come from one of the licensing agencies, most publishers have at least two companies (an ASCAP one and a BMI one). It is wise to negotiate your advance from the licensing agencies before you sign with one company or the other. Your publisher will help arrange the best possible deal for you. By the way, ASCAP stands for American Society of Composers, Authors, and Publishers, and BMI stands for Broadcast Music Incorporated. In theory, ASCAP is owned by the writers and publishers, and BMI is owned by the broadcasters, but in reality they are pretty much equal. There are differences which may be important, depending upon your specific situation, so it is wise to check out all three performing rights societies (ASCAP, BMI, & SEASAC) before you sign. Check out what they have paid in the past on songs that are in your style of writing. More importantly, check out what they can do for *you*.

You can also sign an individual song contract with a publisher, but this is usually not wise unless you are sure he is going to take action on the song. You have to figure that if the publisher has other writers signed to exclusive deals, their material is going to come first. Unless he is really knocked out by your song, it won't have a high priority. A lot depends upon his enthusiasm. If he offers you a single song contract and acts like you're twisting his arm over it, tell him to eat his contract. On the other hand, if he swears he can get immediate action on the tune, let him have a go. The best way to determine his enthusiasm may be money. If the publisher is a reputable one, he should be willing to give you a small advance on the song. Not that a few hundred bucks is going to do you that much good, but it does represent a commitment from the publisher. Remember that it is much better to have someone pushing even one song to name artists than to have your material starring on your brother's cassette player.

You can also ask for a time limit on a single song contract. Rather than sign it away forever, have a clause put in which says if there is no action (recording) of the song within six months, the song reverts back to you. This protects you from the publisher who would take one of your songs merely because he thinks you might one day come up with a legitimate hit, and he wants to have one of your tunes in his catalogue. That sounds flattering, doesn't it? What it actually means is that he intends to use your song for dogpaper until someone else breaks you as a writer. When a writer who has been struggling for a number of years finally hits, there are often publishers coming out of the woodwork with his old songs which they may have done absolutely nothing to promote.

I remember seeing this lady publisher at an important company for about the fifth time, when she went into her "tough bitch" act. I couldn't take her attitude anymore so I started telling her how screwed up I thought she was. All of a sudden, she became real nice, and said she wanted to publish one of my songs. I thought I'd really put her in her place and gotten a song published at the same time. But she had the last laugh, because that song sat in the files for over a year before I was able to get it back. If I had asked for money or a time limit, she would have said no, and I would have saved myself some trouble.

You should be aware of what position you hold on your publisher's priority list. Does he have three projects that are before you, or fifty? You want someone with clout and knowledge to put their time into promoting your material. As a songwriter, you are in the business of getting your songs recorded. There is no value to having fifty songs in your notebook and nothing on record. You can't do it alone, and you can't do it with Bozo the Clown for a publisher. So look until you find the right guy. You have to have confidence in your publisher, and he must have confidence in you. You must feel that you can't wait to get that new song over to him because you know he'll jump on it right away. He has to know that he can depend on you to work at your writing and make it better while you keep bringing him new songs. With the right publisher, songwriting is a dream, but with the wrong one, it is a nightmare.

## Being A Publisher

It's dumb to form your own publishing company unless you really have the power to get songs recorded. It takes considerable finances to adequately demonstrate and promote a song. More importantly, it takes years of establishing contacts in the business. If you're recording an album of your own tunes, which you are financing yourself (known in the business as a "frisbee"), then publish your songs yourself, but realize that you are under many limitations that a reputable publisher can overcome for you.

To form a publishing company, write to ASCAP, BMI, or SESAC and obtain an application. Once you have formed your company, if you expect to receive royalties from record sales, you should obtain the services of the Harry Fox Agency. For a three or four percent fee (depending on your volume), they will collect the money for you. If you have a problem, they will even audit the record label's books if it is necessary to get you fair payment. The Harry Fox Agency is the equalizer between your two bit publishing company and a powerful record label.

After you become an established songwriter, it becomes very wise to form your own publishing company, because now you have the power to get songs to name artists. Successful writers often have their songs co-published by their own company and a well known publisher. In these cases, the writer will usually foot half of the bills, and collect half the publishing profits, while the established publisher does all the work. There is so much profit in publishing the songs of a well known writer that most companies would be happy to do all the work for half the profits.

Being a publisher is more than a license and a name, and many existing publishers should read the following section.

## Knowing It When You Find It

Recognizing a hit song is not as easy as it sounds. The trained ear can sometimes hear a song once, in its roughest form, and realize its potential. To like a song, you have to be psychologically receptive to it when you hear it. If you're in a bad mood, the last thing you may appreciate is a depressing love song, which is okay unless, as a publisher, you just passed on "McArthur Park." On the other hand, if you've been real busy and want to relax, you may not be too receptive to "Whole Lotta Love" by Led Zeppelin. It is a publisher's responsibility to overcome these differences so that he is always attuned to a potential hit.

In general, publishers are looking for light, up tempo songs with a positive outlook on life. That is because these songs are the easiest to get recorded. Many artists write their own material today, and consequently only record songs by other writers if they think they are a hit. That means that most heavy or personal statements wouldn't be recorded by other artists, and most publishers aren't interested in such material. There are exceptions, however, and it is good to remember that a hit song is an indescribable phenomenon. Your goal as a writer or publisher is to develop your ear to the point where you can recognize it when you hear it. In defense of most publishers, they can only be expected to take action on the songs that they feel in their gut are a hit. They know that a lot of the ones they pass on could be hits, but they have to go with their personal feelings because that is the only criteria they've got.

The best way to develop your ability to recognize a hit song is to start analyzing why you like the songs you do. Study the song. How are the lyrics, the melody, the arrangement, the sound of the singer's voice, the guitar, the rhythm, the chorus, the verses, where are the hooks? If you watch the charts try guessing how high a new record will rise, but remember, there are many unseen factors, such as promotion, that help to determine this. After you've been analyzing existing hits for a while, start applying what you've learned to your own songs, or to the material of other writers. Learn to spot when a song is too wordy or when there is a poor musical change between the verse and the chorus. When you hear a song, try to think of what would make it a better one.

Many publishers have become experts in helping writers perfect their material. This can be very subjective, so try to find out what a publisher intends to do with your material before you change it around for him. I went to see this one guy three or four times and kept changing my material the way he advised, until finally he said that the songs were perfect and just the way he liked them. He then told me that he couldn't do anything for me because his office was only dealing in movie themes. Yes, you could say I've had a few frustrating experiences.

## Arrangements

A lot of people are making master quality demos just to push their songs. If a song can't be heard as a hit without the flute part at the end, it probably isn't one. When you are demoing songs, give the artist and producer some room. Don't over-perform it. Publishers, producers, and artists are mainly inter-ested in the hook, the lyrics, and the melody. They have pro-fessional arrangers to do the rest. The arrangement is not that important at this stage unless you intend to record the song yourself. If you have a great idea for the arrangement, you might tell them about it, but first they have to like the song. The greatest arrangement in the world won't sell a song that the listener doesn't like.

If your material is on the order of a Harry Chapin, you may need to do a little arranging so the song can be heard properly, but don't get carried away. Or, if you feel the song *has* to have a two part harmony, you might record the demo that way. The idea is to concentrate on showing off your wares as a writer. A lot of producers have big ego problems and if you come in there trying to show off your arranging capabilities, you may find yourself out the door faster than you came in. You'd be surprised at the people who can be intimidated by someone off the street, so keep it simple.

I've heard of publishers who actually hire people to sing on demos that sound like the artist they are pushing the material to. There was a guy who had a voice like Johnny Cash who made a good living just singing on demos that were going to Johnny's producer.

## Advice To Recording Artists

Up until the Beatles, most artists did not write their own songs. The success of the Beatles prompted many other artists to attempt writing their own material, and many of them succeeded in developing the talent. It is important to recognize your limitations as a songwriter. Maybe you can rectify them with the right partner, but maybe you just don't have a talent for writing songs. More artists have suffered trying to force their songwriting talent than you can imagine. Don't let your desire to make more money or your ego allow you to put your own material on an album when you could record better songs by other writers. The song is far too important for that.

If you are an artist and are having songs submitted to you by publishers and songwriters, you must learn to recognize the songs that are right for you. When you hear a great song, something should happen to you inside. You just get a feeling that you want to sing it. You've got to go by that gut feeling. Listen to advice, but trust yourself. Looking for new tunes is like diving for oysters: there's tons of oysters, but only a few pearls. When you hear a great song, it will sound like it belongs on the radio, even if it's being played on a cigar-box guitar. If you can imagine yourself singing it, then do it.

In a business that is as undefinable as this one, you can't be afraid to take a stand. There are many songs that nobody but the artist and the writer thought could be a hit, but when the record was finished, there was so much honesty and emotion packed into those grooves, there was no stopping it.

## Encouragement

A songwriter has to go through all of the bullshit that a recording artist has to face, but he has fewer areas to master. He really only has to deal with perfecting his songs and finding the right publisher for them, but that doesn't mean that it is any less frustrating. If you have the talent, however, you would be a fool not to pursue it at least long enough to get some professional opinions. Don't give up with your first rejection, but plan on making an objective decision about your talent somewhere along the line. You may not be cut out to be a songwriter, but if you know in your heart that you are, then go for it. You may be a ten year overnight success, but if you love writing songs, it will be worth it. Just remember to keep enjoying it.

# Chapter 5
# The Demo

*"Pick out four of the best originals. Keep them short and to the point. Make sure the vocals come out and only show a brief representation of your instrumental ability. The important thing is to show your originality. The demo must be representative of your sound."*

**—Johnny Sandlin** *

## Demo or Master?

There are demos, demo-masters, and masters. A demo is a demonstration of what you are doing, and there are different levels of that, depending primarily upon who will hear it. If you are doing the demo for yourself, you just want a quick picture of your music. You want as honest a portrayal of your sound as you can get. The purpose is probably either to better your live sound by hearing your mistakes, or else to better enable you to be an objective listener (such as when you record a rough verison of a new tune which you loved writing, only to discover that you hate listening to it).

* *Producer of the Allman Brothers Band, Tim Weisberg, Cher, Bonnie Bramlett and others. Interviewed for the Chicago Daily News by James Riordan.*

If you are doing the demo for a club or an agent in order to get gigs, you want the tape to sound like a hot live act. That means you will have to take more care in preparing and recording it. If you are doing the demo for a label to hear, you'll want to take even more care to get the best possible performance. In this situation you will probably want to do some overdubbing in order to get as clean a sound as possible. It is possible to sell an act with a tape that sounds like it was recorded next to an out-of-tune jack hammer, but that is presuming that someone who listens to fifty tapes a day will put up with the aggravation.

Sometimes an artist will have sufficient connections, or be impressive enough in a live show for a record company to put up some demo-cash. In this case they will advance you five hundred or a thousand dollars to hear what you sound like on tape, and the quality of your original material. This is a prelude to their offering you a contract, so you want to make sure the tape is your best effort.

There is also such a thing as a demo-master. This is when you record a demo on high quality tape (such as, but not limited to, 24 track) and wind up with a performance that you cannot duplicate or exceed. Sometimes you can only capture a certain feeling once and your demo could easily become a master.

A master is just what the term implies. It is the best you can do at a given point in time and space. A master is a forever situation, recorded for release as a record on high quality tape. In that situation, if you don't like what you did, you're going to cringe every time the needle hits the groove. Perfection is unattainable, but a master should be the best you feel you can do.

Any tape that you do on your own, without the backing of a record label, should probably be considered a demo. You can, of course, do master quality demos, but since the release of the record still depends upon interesting a label, you are in a sense making a demo for record companies to hear.

If you have nine or ten dynamite original tunes, you're playing five nights a week to a crowd that goes nuts for you, and your band is as tight as a gnat's ass, then you're probably ready to do a master. But, if you've been together for three months and you think you're the next Rolling Stones, you'd better read this section before you waste a lot of time and money trying to cut a great album when you should be concentrating on cutting your musical teeth.

A lot of new artists are financing their own albums and releasing them on labels like Joe's Records. This is done for three reasons: 1) The artist is dying to see his name on wax and feels that putting out a record represents some sort of milestone in his career. 2) The artist is under the mistaken impression that record companies give more attention to demos that are pressed into records. 3) The artist has a realistic chance of getting airplay and effective distribution.

First of all, a semi-retarded frog can have his own record album if somebody is crazy enough to pay for it. If you spend money to press a record out of your demo, you are paying to have your ego stroked. If you absolutely have to have your face on an album cover, paste your picture over an old James Taylor album and bank the cash you save. In a few instances, artists have been able to get radio airplay from "home releases" sufficient enough to attract attention from major record labels. But this is really an unusual case. You're usually better off putting the money into your act in other ways, such as equipment, promotional material, or even more demos.

The only time it is advisable to press your demo into an album is if you are playing enough gigs to sell enough of these frisbees to make it profitable. That usually means the lounge set where the waitress or somebody can help you stuff these babies down the throats of the unsuspecting patrons. In that case the "album" is getting your name around and making money for you at the same time, so do it. If you are just doing it for exposure, put the money into publicity. Most people don't get too good an impression anyway when they look at the label and see you're recording for "Fishwife Records" or something equally unknown. And record companies are even less impressed. To them it means that, besides being unknown, you are also dumb.

I know guys who are on their third "home released" album. They've more or less chosen to live out a complete fantasy at their own expense rather than go for the reality. It is nice to whip out a couple of your "albums" when your friends are over, but remember, the purpose of an album is to reach the masses. If you're only reaching your mom, dad, and three of your best friends, you might reconsider. And isn't it a little hard to ignore those three thousand unsold albums filling up the hall closet?

The answer to demo or master for a new group is demo. Demo, demo, demo! When your demos start sounding like records, then it's time to consider a master, but not before. Don't press records out of demos and don't take anything other than your best to a record label.

## Recording a Demo

Hold your costs down. A demo is simply a sound picture of where you are, at this particular moment. If you're going into a four track studio at $40 an hour, don't expect to get the same quality you would get at the Record Plant on two inch 24-Track tape with Dolbys and a professional engineer. Most Tascam studios (which are what demo studios usually are) have cheap spring echo and very little effects. They are designed merely to capture your sound on tape rather than enhance it. The reason you do a demo is usually not to show off the sound, but to listen to the tightness, because the tape doesn't lie. To sit there and beat a tune into the ground with thirty takes, when the demo is for your own evaluation is just giving the studio money. You might as well open up your wallet and have them reach right in.

If you are doing the demo to find out your mistakes, don't worry about making it perfect. If you detect some goofs while you're recording, you have less homework to do later, but continue recording the song so you can hear any additional errors.

A quality demo can be made for as little as a few hundred dollars. You must take the attitude that the demo studio is just like the stage. If you can do eight songs in an hour on stage, try to record that many in the same amount of time. Of course it will take you a while to set up and relax in the studio, but once you get going, you shouldn't be stopping very often. You want to hear what you sound like, and "live" recording is the best and the cheapest way. If you are doing the demo for a label, record a good strong instrumental track and then overdub the vocals and lead solos. Make sure the vocals are right and don't get carried away with production. The label wants to hear your sound and material and that's all. John Carter, A & R at Capitol records elaborates: "A demo can be done on a home tape recorder because the technical quality of the home recorder has been upgraded tremendously in recent years. I think a demo should have three tunes on it which don't necessarily have to be the group's most commercial things. The demo should show what the group can do, especially their vocal ability. The vocal performance is about 75% of it."*

One of the best investments that an artist can make is a good four track tape recorder. After you have your equipment and sound system, it should be your number one priority. Spending a thousand bucks on a little system with a six or eight input mini-mixer and four channels can make a big difference in the quality of your sound. It's important to hear where you are if you expect to improve. Train one of your sound men to run the system and record every rehearsal and every show. Do a demo every time you play. Keep the best cuts and edit them together for a good representation of the act.

Note: One good way to purchase a tape deck or anything else for that matter is to set aside a little from each gig in some sort of fund. A "band fund" can be a big help in covering the cost of things like emergency equipment repairs, promotional expenses, and demos. The best way to handle it is to place the money in an account and require every band member's signature to withdraw from the account. This will help keep up the trust level in the band. People can get really squirrely over money. You can spend hours of time helping someone and the moment he thinks he's missing a nickel, he's got a knife to your throat. Playing banker can also help some of the more flakey band members learn about financial matters. You know the ones. They can't understand why their checks are bouncing, because they've still got some blank ones left in their book.

Any demo that you record to present to a record label or manager should be simple and uncluttered. Don't cover up your musical identity with production techniques. Restrict the demo

* © *Chicago Daily News* ("Producers: The Studio Stars" by James Riordon 1/26/78)

to three or four songs, because most people who can help you won't listen to more than that. A demo doesn't have to be single-oriented, but if you have such material, you should definitely include it. More than anything else, the demo has to show what makes your act special.

## Getting A Deal

When you are satisfied that your demo is a good representation of your sound, and your stage act is nearly perfect, you are ready to look for a deal. Getting a deal really depends on how well you have done all the steps that lead up to it. The actual deal can come from anywhere, so there is no particular pattern you should follow in hustling your tape. Before you approach the record labels however, you should approach some of the people who influence them.

The best route would be to get yourself a top flight manager (see Chapter 9: *"Managers, Attorneys, & Agents"*), but this may not be possible. Big time managers are hard to get to, and even harder to impress, but they are worth the effort. As mentioned in Chapter 2, a powerful manager carries a lot of weight with a record label. So, the first thing you do with your demo is get it to established managers.

Be prepared for some difficulty because important managers are rarely interested in new acts. They are usually so busy handling what they already have, they don't have time for new artists. Never-the-less, you shouldn't give up until you've given it a pretty good shot. Find out who manages the important acts and you will find out who are the important managers. By the time you've reached this level, you should know someone who can give you this kind of information. If not, there are ways of finding it out. Often management companies are mentioned on the backs of album covers. In addition, there are some directories available, and special issues of the trades also contain such information. As a last resort, call up the record labels and ask them who manages some of their acts. They'll love you for doing this and they'll love me even more for telling you to do it.

If you are unable to attract a top manager, don't settle for a struggling one. There are other avenues to explore first. Powerful music business attorneys also influence the decisions of the record companies. Read the section on ''A & R'' in Chapter 10 to see how important it is to have a ''well respected source'' on your side. Attorneys who represent major artists are some of the most powerful people in the music business (see Chapter 9). If you can get one of them on your team, getting a deal with a label will be easy. Well, maybe not easy, but at least very possible. Important music attorneys are even harder to locate than managers because they are farther behind the scene. Occasionally they are mentioned in the ''Thanks To'' section on an album cover, but most often you find the good ones through personal contacts.

Some of the major talent agencies also negotiate record contracts, so you might approach them with your demo as well. Basically, any person in a position of real importance can help you get an inside lane to a record company. This includes other recording artists, promoters, producers, engineers, and other people at the label, as well as managers, attorneys, and agents. Not all of these people can help you. Only the ones who are important enough to command the respect of the top people at a record company can do you any good. Don't fall into the trap of thinking that people who work for these people can do the job, because they really aren't in a much better position than you are. Of course, if you can convince the number two man in a top management firm to open some doors for you, do it, but this usually won't happen unless the boss gives his okay.

The best way to promote your demo is to follow your contacts. While it is advisable to first get a good manager, if your brother is in tight with the most powerful music attorney in Hollywood, you might see him first. Go with the important people whom you can get to, but don't give up if you don't have any inside leads. The important thing is to try to get someone influential behind you before you approach a record label. Like most things, you should set aside a reasonable amount of time to pursue this route before abandoning it. I would recommend a few months of good solid effort. If you're still drawing blanks after that, start contacting the labels yourself.

Before we get into this area, let's discuss another point.

## Relocating

Once you have determined that you are ready for the big time, you have to relocate to one of the music centers. In most cases, that means L. A. or New York, although you can also go to Nashville. In fact if you're into country music, you will have more opportunities in Nashville, but you could do it on the coasts as well. Detroit is still a center for R & B, and there is a lot of activity in Chicago, Atlanta, Miami, Philadelphia, Houston, Dallas, San Francisco, Memphis, Seattle, Denver, and other areas. If you can't move to any of these places, it doesn't mean that you won't succeed, but it does mean that your chances become much less. Not only do few labels or managers listen to all the tapes that come in the mail, but not living in the music centers denies you opportunities in other ways.

The way to find out about big shot lawyers and other such necessary information is through friends in the business. The people on the street who are hustling their talents in the same way you are can be your most valuable source of information. When you live in one of the music centers, you have the tremendous advantage of making contacts in many additional ways. The guy at the supermarket has a friend in the music business who turns out to be an idiot, but he introduces you to this chick who used to go out with Bob Seger's attorney. She dumps you after two dates, but you meet a guy named Mario with her at the disco and he knows a girl in promotion for Columbia. All of these people may lead you nowhere, but sooner or later you might meet someone who is legit and who likes your music. Besides, the experience and little tidbits you pick up by going through this maze can also be very valuable. Just don't get caught up chasing the pie-in-the-sky that the local lunies offer you. You know. Keep an eye out for reality.

Another big advantage to living in a music city is that everything you need to pursue your art is easier to obtain. You can get better deals on instruments, session musicians and studio time (you can rent time in a 16 Track studio in L.A. for as little as $40 an hour with no problem). In addition, there are countless courses open to you in every aspect of the music business, and you can find the players and song writers you need just by scanning the papers. In a music center like L.A., New York, or Nashville, it's all there if you want to look for it. And if you're really serious about this business, you should be there too. As soon as you get a bite from a manager or label, you'll probably wind up moving anyway and, once you're ready, the sooner you relocate, the faster you'll get something happening. Sure, it's scary to pack up and head out for the big city sometimes, and it's much easier to wait until you've got something definite waiting for you. But that might never happen. I told you it was a gamble, so roll the dice.

Taking your tapes to record companies is not that difficult. Getting someone to listen to them is a little harder and getting someone important to hear them is a lot harder. The person you want to impress is the Director of A & R (see this section in Chapter 10), but others in that department can help you too. There are a lot of flunkies in this area so expect a run-around. Without an "in", there is nothing you can do except take what they dish out. Many companies will refuse to listen to your tape while you are present. So leave it with them. After all, a slim chance is better than no chance. Presumably you've already protected the material, so what can you lose. There are some people who would tell you that "delivering" a tape to a label can damage your image, but if you don't have an "in" there, you don't have an image to damage.

Hit the big labels first and then the smaller ones. Don't wait on anybody. It's better to have two offers than one anyway, so get as many tapes out as fast as you can. When you're totally unknown, the first thing you want to do is to get somebody interested in you. It's not advisable to sign with a label that operates out of a garage or something equally smalltime, because they probably won't be able to do you any good. Sometimes, however, getting an album out is better than just sitting, but weigh your choices very carefully.

When you're talking to people at the record companies, don't be overeager, but don't act bored either. You've got something that you think will make them a lot of money. If they disagree, you'll just move on to another company. That's all. Be professional (see "The Deal" in Chapter 11). Every time you record a new demo, or when anything significant changes in your music, you can see everybody again. After a while you'll know who to see and who is a waste of time.

Remember that there are plenty of labels out there and don't get discouraged by negative answers until you've thoroughly scouted the field. I know some guys who give up after seeing two or three labels. They make ten demos and start five new bands every year. Some of my most discouraging and embarrassing moments have been spent sitting across the desk from an A&R person. Don't let it get you down. In fact, reread *"The Golden Reel-To-Reel & The Platinum Turntable Myth"* in Chapter 1 before you begin pushing your tape.

While you're contacting labels, don't let your act become stagnant. Rehearsals and performances have to keep going on because the first thing the label will want to do if they like your tape is see your stage show. Try to view hustling your tapes as just another part of the process. It could lead to a payoff, but it might just lead you to more work and a better perspective. It will probably take a few trips around the horn with new demos before you finally make a big connection.

It is difficult to give you a step-by-step direction here, because there are so many factors that come into play. You may get a producer, manager, or attorney before you get a record deal, or you may get them after. The next section of this book will deal with the actual process of making a record. After this we will further discuss the business side of music.

# Chapter 6
# The Producer & Picking A Studio

*"There are three things I'm going for in the studio. One is a hit record. Two is to deliver to the record company what they expect me to deliver, and three is to turn a lot of people on by capturing what the artist is really trying to do. I try to produce each record so that it will last for years to come.*

**—Paul Leka***

## The Producer & What He Does

The producer is responsible for your recorded sound. His primary function is to take the best of what you do and get it on tape in its most creative and accessible form. He helps you locate and select material, he picks the studio, chooses the engineer, directs the session, and mixes the final product.

In the movie business, the producer is the man with the money who either pays for everything or finds people to put up the cash. He oversees all the business operations of the film. In the record business this person is called the executive producer of the album, not the producer. The producer of an album is analogous to the director of a film. The director of a movie

*Producer of Harry Chapin, Gloria Gaynor, REO and others © Chicago Daily News ("Producers: The Studio Stars" by James Riordan 1/26/78)

is the guy who co-ordinates all the creative elements and makes the film happen. In music the producer is the man who makes the record happen.

In the beginning, he helps you locate your tunes through publishers and writers, or he can work with songs you've written and help you decide which ones to record. If he thinks some of your material needs to be rewritten, he may advise you or even help you do it. It is the producer's responsibility to narrow down your material to the absolute best songs. He provides you with the objective voice that every artist (especially a new one) needs. Obviously, you must have confidence in him to trust him with this responsibility.

The producer puts the various elements of a recording session together. He probably has favorite studios and engineers that he likes to work with, but he should also listen to your suggestions in these areas. It is his responsibility to line up the right studio musicians if you need them, and determine what rates to pay them. He should know where to get the best deals on instrument rentals, what arrangers to use for string and horn charts, what background singers to hire, and all the other components necessary to make great records.

The producer is the captain of the ship. When you walk inside the studio, he calls the shots. Part of his job is to keep things flowing throughout the session, and that means balancing egos, tempers, and artistic sensitivity in a way that is both harmonious and productive. If things aren't going well in a particular session, the producer must know when to call it a night. He's got to know when he's not going to get anymore and not be afraid to hit the off switch. That ability, in itself, can be very important to bringing the album in within the allowed budget and not suffering to do it.

The producer's goal is to bring the project to a finished piece of work on vinyl. He lives with the record from meeting the artist and working with his material, to the final responsibilities of mixing and mastering. In some cases, the producer is also the executive producer, in that he finances the record and hustles the deal. He is the quarterback of the whole show. The name of the game is to get it on tape, and the producer must do whatever it takes to make that happen.

## Where To Find Him & Picking The Right One

Most producers are easily reachable through the studios or record labels where they have worked. If you see a producer's name on the back of an album, call the studio where the record was made, or the label which released it, and they should be able to put you on to him. If the producer has his own production company, it will usually be listed in the yellow pages under production or record companies. The directory at the back of this book lists several top producers, but if the one you want is not there, track him down through the companies with which he has been associated.

The best way to decide what producers you like is to listen to a lot of records. Go by the general sound. If you like the records, you probably like the production. If you like three or four things by the same producer, you can almost be sure of it.

After you locate a producer you want to work with, you have to set up a meeting with him. Most producers won't get involved with someone who is unsigned. If they do, they will probably want to sign the band to their production company and then lease them to a label. Most producers, however, won't want to take the chance that they might wind up working for nothing, or even losing money on the project. From their point of view, why should they risk working with an unsigned act, when they can be guaranteed good money for other projects.

If you are already signed and looking for a producer, you'll want to set up a meeting to listen to his latest efforts and play him some of your tunes. Some guys play hard to get ("If I get a chance, I'll come out and see your act" etc). Usually the best way to know if a producer is genuinely interested in working with you is by his reaction when he saw you perform. If, during your show, he spilled fourteen drinks down the front of his chest because he was too drunk to realize that you were doing a good job, then he is not your man. The same is true if he spent more time hitting on the waitresses at the club than hearing your set. If a producer is genuinely interested in your sound, he'll talk to you about it. He'll have some constructive criticism, and you should be able to recognize his enthusiasm. Things like "It's nice, but I'm really busy right now . . . after I get through with the 73 projects I've got on the line, however, maybe we can give it a shot" are not signs of genuine enthusiasm. Like everything else, it is a matter of priority. If he really likes it, he will want to do it.

Most likely you will be going after a producer with an impressive track record. A brand new producer may do just as good a job, but you probably won't want to take a chance on him (would you get into a 747 with a pilot who just got out of Cessna Training School?). It is important that you do not get overenthralled with a name, however. Sometimes bands go after a name, even when the producer has had no experience with their type of music. If the guy has produced nothing but folk hits all of his life and you want to sound like Led Zeppelin, I think you're in the wrong place, no matter how big a name he has. Another bad thing about going after a "name" producer is that they are going to want your left lung, arm, and big toe thrown in with the deal. And even then you might have to wait for a year until he has time to do the project.

You want a guy who produces music that is similar to what you want to do. You also want someone whom you can get along with and feel comfortable around. You don't want somebody who intimidates you. No one can work well when they're intimidated, particularly if they are trying to be creative. You have to feel good about your producer and respect his word. He should inspire confidence in you and be sensitive to your music. You should feel that you can trust him with your future because that is exactly what you are doing. More than anything else, it's the rapport. You'll know when it's right.

## Building Rapport

After you've agreed on a producer, you want to spend some time building your rapport with him before you go into the studio. A lot of building rapport is picking the producer's brain and letting him pick yours. You know, the fine art of conversation. Talk to him about your music. Ask him what he really thinks of your songs. Now that you've agreed to work together, you can be more honest and direct with each other. How does he like your lyrics, your sound, what are his suggestions for improving them? How should you arrange things in the studio, should you use a three part harmony or a two part on this one song, should you use a piano or a clavinet? Tell him your ambitions, what artists you respect, and where you see your music going. Get to know each other.

## Fees

Like all areas in the music business, a producer's fee can vary and is negotiable. If he's coming off of a big hit record, he may demand thirty, forty, or even fifty grand from the label and four or five points on the album (the bigger you become in this business, the more you will hear about points. Everybody wants more points. It's kind of like a basketball game, except you're the ball. Points are percentages of profit. If your producer has four points on the record, then he will get 4% of the gross earnings after all production costs have been paid back to the label).

Most producers charge by the side, which means they do it on a per song basis. There are no standards here in the absolute sense, but the average ranges from a thousand to fifteen hundred per side. That means you can't expect to get an experienced, first-rate producer to do your album for less than ten to fifteen thousand dollars. He will probably want at least three points as well. You must understand that you're asking for three or four months of his life in many cases. It isn't just the time in the studio. There are all kinds of meetings with the label and the artist, pre-production work, post production work, and the responsibility of worrying about the record from the day he agrees to do it to the day it hits the streets. He earns his money.

## Changing Producers

Never change producers in the middle of a project unless you are prepared to start over completely. You can't expect one man to pick up where another left off, because every producer works in a little different way. One of the most important steps in producing is the selection of material, and that occurs first.

Nobody can produce a good record if he doesn't like some of the material on it, so you have to start over from the top.

After you've done a few albums, changing to another producer can be very healthy. Once you know your way around the studio and have a few projects under your belt, it might be good to get a different perspective. If you haven't achieved what you've been looking for in the studio, then you *should* make a change.

If you have a good thing going, however, don't get picky and mess it up. If you've had a couple of successful albums with the same guy behind the board, don't tamper with that combination. Keep the team together. The greatest way to blow something is to break up a team once it starts rolling. Sometimes popular artists change producers for selfish reasons. They have a big enough name now that they can bring in someone else under a new agreement that is more profitable to them. If you've been successful with the guy you're replacing, that is letting greed get in the way of your career. If you haven't been successful with him, it is good business to change.

The size of the artist has a lot to do with it. Neil Diamond worked with Tom Catalano on something like ten albums. That's a long time to work with anybody. After ten albums, Neil decided to produce himself and he is still very successful. You can't say that Tom Catalano didn't help Neil Diamond, and you can't say that Neil didn't help Tom. It was just time for a change.

Artists often change producers to expand their creative influence over the album. This can be a mistake, because an artist needs that objective voice. You want someone in there with you who isn't afraid to tell you when you are getting out of line. The difference between creativity and excess is knowing when to stop.

## Being A Producer

It takes experience. Trial and error is what makes a good producer, but there are certain things that you need to know. You need to know a little about studio technique. You don't have to be an engineer and know all the knobs and dials backwards and forwards, but you should be familiar with the board. Producers usually come from engineering or musical backgrounds. If you have been an engineer, you'll have no problems in this area, but if you haven't, you will have to learn the technical things behind getting certain sounds on the board. If you can't explain what you want to your engineer, you can't expect him to get it for you.

You also have to know about music, especially what makes music sound the way it does. That means being familiar with the sounds of many musical instruments and the impact that certain sounds have upon a given part in a song. The producer doesn't necessarily have to play a musical instrument or read music, but he must have an affinity to musical sound and know that it takes a little bit more than hiring a studio and an engineer to get that sound on tape.

It would also behoove a producer to know a little about promotion, marketing, management, accounting, image, and everything else that affects the sales of records. Besides his work in the studio, the producer usually has to function as an independent businessman, so he must know a little about business. Some producers learn this the hard way. The best way to invest your money is not into a Porsche, a Jaguar, and a houseboat, but it is best not to give it all to Uncle Sam either. In the beginning, therefore, at least learn some simple bookkeeping and expand your business knowledge as your income increases.

A producer has to have a strong personality without being overbearing. He must encourage the artist's suggestions and use some of them, while passing on others. The best producers are the ones who are able to say "no." They won't go along with anything that can happen in that studio. If they don't like it, they say no, because they know that their name is going on that record, and the more junk that comes out with their name on it, the less income they will earn. At the same time, they never intimidate the artist. They want to know the artist's ideas, because it is his music they are capturing on tape, and even if he is inexperienced, his ideas may be instinctively good. A good producer is like a father to the artist. He lets him do his thing and he also tells him where to get off.

## In The Studio

The producer usually will not run the controls on the board unless he wants to get a specific sound. Sometimes handling the knobs can make you more *aware* of the sound, but the board is usually the engineer's responsibility. In the studio, the producer's job is to listen. The guy has got to have the ears of a hawk. If he hears an unbalanced vocal blend, he has to tell one of the singers to back off the mic a few inches. If one of the singers is out of tune, it is the responsibility of the producer to tell him so. Sometimes a singer can't hear when he's out of tune and he might argue about it. The best thing to do in that case is to play back the tape for him. If he still can't hear it, tell him you'll put him down for the Beltone Award and move on.

The engineer is very important to the producer. A good engineer makes his job a lot easier. Ted Templeman, producer of The Doobie Brothers, Van Morrison, Carly Simon, Little Feat, Nicolette Larson, and Van Halen, describes his relationship. "My engineer, Donn Landee, helps me greatly in the studio. We've worked so long together that now we instinctively know what each other wants before anything is said. This is a tremendous help in getting the session done the way it should be done. I rely on Donn a great deal."*

It takes a lot off the producer's shoulders to know that the engineer has his end together. The producer is dealing with the song, the performance, and all the other aspects of the session, so it's important to know that things like microphone placements are going to be right. A good engineer is a producer's right arm. If the producer has to play with the drum sound for a couple of hours because it sounds like the kick drum is made out of cardboard, he's got problems. If you're producing at a studio that you haven't worked in before, and working with an engineer who has a pair of bricks for ears, it's all over but the crying.

The producer must define whatever it was that he first liked about the act and then capture it on tape. He must translate and emphasize that subtle quality throughout the record. Ron Nevison, producer and engineer, who has worked with the

* © *Chicago Daily News* ("Producers: The Studio Stars" by James Riordan 1/26/78)

Rolling Stones, The Who, Bad Company, Barbara Streisand, Dave Mason, The Babys, and Led Zeppelin, comments on what he tries to achieve in the studio. "I use the record to paint as interesting a picture of the artist as I can. I try to pick up the slack in the studio and make the adjustments to round it out and make it as complete as possible."*

Getting the most out of an artist can sometimes be very difficult. Some artists start to freak out two weeks before going into the studio. No matter how much they've rehearsed, they still feel unprepared. A lot of great performing artists can't cut it in the studio. They need to feel that vibration coming back from the audience. When you get an artist like that, the first thing you do is cry. After that, you do whatever it takes to simulate the rush he gets from the stage. If he gets high or drinks before he goes on stage, let him do it before he sings in the studio. If he needs people to play to, load the studio up with folks. It's the producer's responsibility to get a great vocal performance out of that artist and he must do whatever it takes. If you've got an artist who knocks you out live, but in the studio he sings like he belongs at "Bob & Dotty's Lounge," you have to do something about it. If he needs to sing on the balcony facing the ocean, call up the Wally Heider mobile sound truck and arrange it.

If there is nothing a producer can do to get the kind of performance he wants out of an artist, he has to recognize that. In other words, there is a time to punt. You can only do a song so many times, and then it gets crazy. It's the producer's responsibility to get the best performance he can from the artist *without going over budget.* You can blow an entire budget on one song if you get carried away with perfection. The producer has to be conscious of the time and money he is spending in the studio. He should never pressure the artist in this respect, but at the same time, he must keep things moving.

The more you are in a studio, the better you will get. A producer, even more than an artist or an engineer, needs to work with different artists because he will learn something new with each one. Ted Templeman elaborates: "Van Morrison is hard to produce because he is highly creative and changes his mind a

* © *Chicago Daily News ("Producers: The Studio Stars" by James Riordan 1/26/78)*

lot. Lowell George was also a creative genius, but he had definite ideas about what he wanted. The Doobie Brothers are difficult in another way. They're all different personalities, but they all have equal input, so their difficulties are usually deciding amongst themselves rather than disagreeing with me. Each act is different."*

Some producers only relate to hard rock, others only to MOR (hip slang for "middle of the road" which is unhip slang for easy listening music), others only to disco, and still others only to country. But there are some producers who relate to hard rock, MOR, disco, country, and Dick Contino on the accordian. Some guys can produce anything. It's good not to let yourself be typecast into a particular bag of music if you have the ability to produce other types as well. A lot of producers have to accept work that is not necessarily their bag, but they're professional enough to pull it off. It all depends on his musical tastes and how badly he wants to work. If he can afford to wait around for the next Led Zeppelin, more power to him, but if he needs to eat once in a while, he might have to take on some other work.

## Starting Out

To be a producer, you have to have something to produce. So look for an act that excites you, and realize that you are going to make a lot of mistakes the first few times out. Everybody does. Producing is trial and error and learning from the experience. Being around people in the business, especially other producers, can really shortcut your learning time. The more time you spend around a studio, the better. Other than having that innate ability to hear sound quality, and the love of music to want to capture it on tape, there isn't any real magic to it. If you want to be a producer, you need to know a little about studios and a little about music. And a lot of experience.

## Picking A Studio: What To Look For

*"I look at recording and live performance as two different concepts. I want to do the best I can in the studio, so I*

---

* *Ibid*

*don't consider the live performance until I'm all through*
*recording. Then I decide if I want to play the song live and*
*how I should do it. When we're making a record, that's*
*all we're doing. We're not thinking of the past or the*
*future.''*

**—Robin Trower***

Once you are ready to do a master recording, you need to pick
out the right studio. There are certain things to look for. Rather
than what to *look* for, maybe I should say what to *feel* for,
because the most important thing in selecting a studio is finding
one that makes you feel good. To borrow a term from "The
Brian Wilson Pop Handbook To West Coast Sixties Culture,"
the *"vibrations"* are very important. Not the vibrations per deci-
bal or some such garbage, but the vibrations laid on your head.
When you're talking about making good quality records, most
of the studios you would consider are pretty much the same
from a technical standpoint. They all buy their equipment from
the same companies and the technical variations in their quality
could only be understood by an engineer.

There are different kinds of tape, for example. You can use
3M, Scotch, or Ampex. And you can record at plus five, or at
plus four, which is the amount of sound that you are sending
onto the tape. But if your act isn't really cooking in the studio,
all of that means zero. If you aren't comfortable playing there,
all that technical magic is really going to waste. So look for a
good vibe.

If you're doing a demo, none of this is as important as it is
when you are making a record. A demo studio can be held
together by bailing wire and chewing gum, and it will still work
as long as when the red light goes on, you get a demo back. But
many demos have been blown by unnecessary tension as well.
If you don't feel good about a place, it won't sound as good as
it could.

A recording studio is not just state-of-the-art design and equipment. A studio is people as well (for the record, I think state-
of-the-art is a disgustingly hip term which I promise not to use

* © *Rock-Pop, 10/23/77*

more than ten times in this book and that is less than you'll find it mentioned in any *chapter* of most books about sound recording). The vibes from the people at the studio are nearly as important as the vibes of the studio itself. Of course your relationship with your producer and your engineer are the most important (see sections in this chapter on "The Engineer" and "The Producer"), but you also need to feel good about the second engineer and the overall attitude of the studio personnel.

Don't be intimidated by the beautiful plants, the big speakers, the sexy girls, the fantastic equipment, or the ultra hip design of the furniture. You're not there to impress the owners of the studio or anyone else. You're still the client, whether it is your first or fiftieth time. Most of the people you come in contact with at a first rate recording studio should be ready, willing, and able to bend over backwards to please you. They want you to be a happy client. Even if the record you cut there never becomes a monster hit on the charts, you are still a client who is going to go out and tell people how you were treated.

Look at the physical design. Is it something that you can feel comfortable playing in? The design of some studios work against their objective. One of the first studios that I worked in had the artist in a sort of pit about twenty feet *below* the control booth. The producer and the engineer looked *down* on the artist from the control room. It was so intimidating that it was impossible for a new artist to feel comfortable there.

## What To Listen For

The sound is the next most important thing you want in a studio, and the best way to check that out is through your own ears. Ninety-nine percent of the time you won't know enough about technical engineering or studio qualifications, so base your decision on the sound that you've heard coming out of that studio. Listen to the product that has been done there. Make sure that you listen to it both at home and in the studio so you can get an idea of the difference between the studio speakers and a home playback system. There are a lot of things that sound incredible on those huge studio monitors, but when you get them home, they sound like last year's cat. *This is very important.* I've heard many records that sound fabulous in the studio, but at home they sound like burps. That's why you need to get records that have been done there, which you can take home (yes, even if you have to buy them, cheapskate. You're only talking about a forty thousand dollar investment in studio time. It ought to be worth risking a few bucks). You need to hear the sound of that studio on something that you are used to listening on. If you go by what you hear in the studio, you are going to get psyched out every time.

Also, don't make the mistake of thinking that you are going to get exactly the same sound with a different engineer. A different engineer can make the same studio sound totally different. You should go with the engineer who did the things you like at that studio if that is possible. If you have your own engineer, have him listen with you and help you make the decision. Of course a lot of these decisions will be made by your producer, but it's good to know about it even if you aren't producing yourself.

High rates do not necessarily mean good sound. It does not follow that the more expensive a studio is, the better its sound. Once again, let me remind you not to be impressed by cosmetics. Some of the big time rock studios are so slick you feel like you stumbled into a Paris fashion show. Don't let the looks throw you. A pretty girl can be the most vicious person you'll ever meet. It's the same with studios. A pretty studio might sound like a litter box the day after the cat ate a roll of tin foil. Just because the studio has pinball machines, saunas, jacuzzies, and lots of pretty girls running around, does not mean it sounds good. Believe it or not, you're not there to take saunas and jacuzzies with pretty girls. You're there to make a record. Don't lose sight of your objective.

## The Engineer

A studio is merely a camera. A fantastic Nikon camera in the hands of an unprofessional user will only turn out average pictures, but if you put that same camera in the hands of a pro, he'll give you pictures that will blow your mind. It's the same with a studio. A studio takes pictures of sound and you'd better make damn sure that you have a professional behind the controls.

I can't overemphasize the importance of the engineer. The greatest equipment in the world will sound like a cheap demo room in the hands of an inept engineer. You can't make a professional record without a professional engineer. When you are talking with a prospective engineer, find out who he's worked with and what kind of music he's into. Is he into your music? If you know anything about sound, ask him how he mics the drums, does he like to mic the bass or run it direct, what are his little tricks? Ask yourself if you feel good about the guy. Can you handle working with the guy for three hundred hours or so?

Like everything else, when it comes to the engineer, you will usually get what you pay for, so don't try to skimp. A good engineer can cost anywhere from $25 to $50 an hour. Some of the great ones can command even a higher price, but you should be able to find the person you need for $25 an hour.

Build a rapport with your engineer. *Talk* to him. Once you've established a rapport, you'll feel more comfortable with him, and that affects the whole studio situation. A lot of the uptightness in the studio is caused by all the uptightness one feels with the individuals in the room, and most of that can be straightened out before the session. If the artist and the engineer don't have a rapport, the artist usually suffers. When you and the engineer do not understand each other, he will probably wind up doing everything his own way. His way may be good, but it may not be right for you. If he understands you, he can use his talent to get what *you* want and that's what you're paying him for. Equally important is the fact that when you feel confident with your engineer, you'll listen to him. That's very important because he's the man who can get you through the pitfalls of the studio, especially if you're a beginner.

## Being An Engineer

In the last five years, the artistic knowledge and true importance of the engineer has really come to light. He can make an
average act sound great, and a great act sound fabulous. It takes
training and perseverance to be a good engineer. It's a lot of
hard work just getting to the point where you can handle a job
if you can get one. You have to want it.

If you want to become an engineer, you probably like both
music and electronics. You can like one more than the other,
but you are going to have to deal effectively with both. You
are in the only aspect of the music world that is as technical as
it is creative (session players and music attorneys run a close
second). You have to develop the ability to be technically aware
of what is going on, while being open to creative ideas. You
must be able to be as creative electronically as the artist is
musically, but that is not your goal. Your goal is to get his sound
down on tape in the best way possible.

There are several good courses in sound engineering being
offered in many recording studios. If you live in a major city,
you might check out this possibility.* There are many good
books on the subject, and one magazine that should both teach
and entertain you is "Recording Engineer & Producer." The
only real way to learn to be an engineer however, is to do it.
Just being around the atmosphere of a studio can really help
you. A great opportunity lies in becoming a second engineer
and helping to set up and work the sessions. The best procedure
is to get as much training as you can on your own, and then start
using it in any capacity that you can.

Don't think that by going to engineering school you will get
a job. You are there to gain knowledge, not a job position.
Unfortunately, many such schools imply that once you have
completed your course, getting the job will be a mere formality.
It's not that easy. Once again, you have to make a decision. If
you really want to be an engineer, you may have to move to
Los Angeles, New York, or Nashville. There are a few other
recording centers, but these are the main three. In the same

* See Appendix 6

way an artist must make the jump when he feels he is ready, so must the engineer. If you want to be an engineer, you have to go through much of the same bull that an aspiring recording artist has to face. There's a lot of competition. You have to work for free before you get paid, you have to knock on a lot of doors, and when your shot comes, you have to have the guts to take it.

The best way to get a position as a first engineer is to start as a second engineer, but even getting that job requires a lot of persistence. You've got to contact the studios. Not just the great ones, but all of them that can afford to pay you a salary. Make your presence known as much as you can without making a pest of yourself. Often a second engineer gets hired because, at four in the morning, someone remembers him coming around the studio asking for work. When your phone rings in the middle of the night because the regular second is sick or something, recognize that as your shot, and *take it.*

The job of second engineer is a hard one. He's the person who everyone forgets to introduce, and those who remember, forget his name. There is very little glory and money in being a second engineer. The salary pays the rent and that's about all. The workload, however, can be tremendous, sometimes requiring a commitment of sixty to eighty hours a week. You are the first to arrive at a session and the last one to leave. When you're dead tired and the session is finally over, you might have to stay another two hours to make tape copies and clean up the studio. Just remember that you are there to get experience, and you won't be there forever.

After you've been a second for a while, you will start getting opportunities to do some first engineering, usually on the sessions that nobody else wants to do. As you prove yourself behind the board, more opportunities will come your way. Your career might go something like this: After pounding the pavement in L.A. for three months, you get your first job, as a cleanup man at "Tin Sound" Studios. You're sure this must be one of the ten lowest positions in the sound industry and still you are overworked. After a month or so, one of the second engineers at "Tin Sound" gets his thumb caught in a fader and you take his place. After getting four months more experience under your belt, you land a job with "Pie In The Sky" records as a second engineer. Six months later you become a full-fledged first engineer at "Pie In The Sky" and from there, the pies the limit . . . I mean the sky's the limit. The better you get, the better jobs you can command.

As an engineer you will have to get along with people. You can have all of the technical knowledge in the world, but if you haven't learned how to establish a rapport with people, you won't get to use it. Understanding and having good communication with an artist and his producer is part of your job. An artist is not always the most articulate person in the world when it comes to explaining what kind of sound he wants. To decipher what he means by descriptions like a "purple guitar sound" or a "funky bass" requires some effort on your part. You also need to communicate back to him in language that he understands. Contrary to popular belief, engineers are not paid to spout off technical jargon that nobody else in the session understands. They are paid to *communicate* and get the sound on tape.

Usually only those who are really into the music business realize the value and talent of a good engineer. That means that most of your family and friends will not share the excitement and sense of romance you feel at becoming a top engineer. After the fourth person asks you what railroad you drive for, you will understand this a lot better. Some of the people who buy records will adore you, but others never read the album credits. Don't let it get you down. Just because an engineer has a low public profile, in no way does that lessen his important contribution to the business of making records. People aren't paid thirty or forty dollars an hour for being unimportant.

## Rates & Recording For Free

When you are looking for a studio to record your album, you have got to be very cognizant of what you are paying. Too many artists don't pay close enough attention to the rates and they wind up going over budget. All rates are negotiable, and if a studio tells you their rates are firm, tell them goodbye and go find one who will negotiate. All the big studios negotiate to some degree, so don't feel you're being unprofessional by asking for a lower rate. On the contrary, by protecting your interests, you are being very professional. A first rate 24-Track studio is going to cost between $100 and $150 per hour and that may not include the engineer. You want to get the best deal you can, but you don't want to sacrifice quality.

Recording for free refers to a couple of things. The first is that, in the beginning stages of your career, you are going to have to give away your talent on many occasions to get something important back. When you help someone out by playing on their demo, you are not only helping them, but yourself as well. What you get in return is the "Big E,"—experience, and believe me it is worth its weight in gold. Too many people in this nutty business are afraid to help each other. Don't look at it as if you're being taken advantage of, when in fact you could use the experience. There's nothing wrong with recording for free as long as the person you're helping isn't exploiting your talent to make money (If he is exploiting you, he is stealing. I remember this one unknown English artist who asked several of his better known friends to play "anonymously" on his album. They agreed, but when the album came out, they were all advertised on the front cover. He used their names to sell his album without their consent). There may be some risk, but if you deny yourself all the experience gained by playing for free, you are the one who suffers.

Trading talent for exerience is also good for beginning engineers and producers. A lot of mutually beneficial projects never get off the ground because the people involved are too jaded or paranoid to help each other out. It's gotten to the point in L.A. that when you form a new band, half the musicians expect you to pay them while they're deciding whether they want to join it or not. If you're going to play on somebody's demo, or sing backup on a home album, or engineer a tape of new songs being pushed to publishers, or whatever, make an agreement with the person you're helping, so that if he scores big with the project you will get some monetary compensation. That way, you're protected and you won't be taken advantage of. Believe me, the experience pays off and there will come a time when you need some free help on a project as well. "Play on other's demos as you would have them play on yours."

The second meaning of the term "recording for free" refers to not being charged for studio time. Unless your dad owns a recording studio, the only way you will experience this is through "spec time." A lot of studios will give away recording time on a speculation basis. "Spec time" is used to fill the gaps at the studio when it is not being used. With the exception of the engineer and the tape, it costs almost as much to operate an empty studio as one which is in use. If the studio believes in your talent, they may allow you to record for the cost of the tape and the engineer, on the condition that if you land a deal, you will pay them for the time and record the rest of your project there.

Spec time is a great deal if you can get it. Getting it depends on the amount of talent you have and your rapport with that particular studio. The entrepreneur of that studio has got to believe in your talent and ability to get the deal. You've got to believe in the studio and have enough guts to ask for the spec time.

Most big studios will allow some spec recording during their down time, and almost all of them have down time. That might mean you will be recording from 2 a.m. to 6 a.m. on Sunday nights until you complete the project, but if you can handle the schedule, it's worth it. A spec deal may turn into a fifteen or twenty thousand dollar account for the studio, so it's worth it to them. They are still paying all their bills when the studio is empty, and if you cut a hit there, it will bring in all kinds of business for them. So ask! The worst that can happen is they will say no. They shouldn't think any less of you for it, and if they do, you don't want to deal with them anyway.

If the studio agrees to give you some spec time, ask them if you can bring in your own engineer. Make sure that you have someone who can do the job before you ask. Don't turn over a quarter of a million dollar studio to a "soundman." If you do have a good engineer who will work on spec for you, then your only cost will be the tape. That means you'll be getting something like $2,400 worth of recording for a hundred bucks or so. Not bad.

Basically, everyone in this business is a talent scout, and studios are no different. Obviously, they can't give spec time to everybody, so they have to be very choosey. If a studio turns you down for spec time, you shouldn't feel slighted or refuse to record there in the future. They may believe in your talent, but doubt your ability to get a deal. That is the prime reason for turning down spec time. So, don't take it personally.

The recording that you do on spec is designed for release, so it has to be the best work you are capable of doing. If you get a deal with tapes that were done on spec, you are responsible for reimbursing the studio for the time at their normal rate. Of course there are a thousand different deals you can make with the studio, including giving them a piece of your publishing, time payments, or your first born child. If, for some reason, you sign with a label and they want you to record the rest of the project at another studio, you can always work out an agreeable compensation with the studio that gave you the spec time.

The first time you record in a professional studio can be really intimidating. The space age electronics and walls of gold records can make you feel like you don't belong. So make sure you pick a place that is as comfortable as you can find. The bottom line is that you are looking for a good feeling from the place. It is where you are going to be working and creating so the atmosphere must be conducive to creativity. You must like the sound and the people. You need a professional engineer and you need to have a rapport with him. More than anything else, you need to remember that you are there to make music, and everything involved must contribute, rather than detract, from that goal.

# Chapter 7
# Preparing For The Studio

*"I believe in as much advance preparation as possible, especially at today's studio rates. I may not use formal arrangements, but I will use rehearsals so everybody knows exactly what they're going to do before the session."*
**—John Carter** *

### Saving Money and Time

The best place to rehearse is not in the studio. That may come as a real shock to those artists who *begin* an album project in the studio rather than record what they have already prepared. Some guys come into the session with two chord changes and half a verse of lyrics and figure they can get the rest of the material together in the studio. Wrong.

A studio is like a camera. A great photographer might take four hours to set up a shot and only ten minutes to shoot it. Recording should be approached in the same manner. Choosing the material, arranging it, learning the arrangements, and re-working the arrangements, and reworking the arrangements

---

*A&R at Capitol and producer of Bob Welch and Sammy Hagar © Chicago Daily News ("Producers: The Studio Stars" by James Riordan 1/26/78)

again, should all be done *before* the session. Make damn sure that the songs sound just the way you want them to before you set foot in the studio. Do all this work in a rehearsal hall at $10 an hour or less instead of in a studio that costs something like $150 an hour.

Most people make the mistake of thinking they are more prepared than they actually are. They think if they practice the songs anymore they will die from boredom, but when they get into the studio and really hear themselves, they begin to have a lot of doubts. The problem is that they are not really listening to themselves in rehearsal. They keep making the same mistakes over and over again without realizing it until they hear them booming back over those big studio monitors. Try to *listen* during rehearsals. It is even better to tape rehearsal sessions and listen to a bit of each song as you prepare for the studio. Remember, the tape is your most objective listener, because it can't lie.

The better prepared you are, the more time and money you will save. Take plenty of care during prerecording rehearsal sessions. Plan your rehearsals to cover every aspect of the studio. You can even tape your overdubs so that you can make sure they're right. Preparation will save you all kinds of time, money, and exasperating moments. While the meter is running, you'd better have your act together.

Know exactly what you will need in the studio and don't assume anything. Figure out what instrumentation you are using for each song, and what additional instruments you will require. What is available through the studio and what will you have to rent? Where is the best place to rent them? You'd better reserve any instruments that you have to rent in plenty of time before the session. It is unwise to plan on using any instrument in the studio if you aren't totally familiar with it. You need to practice with even the simplest instrument before recording. You'd be surprised how weird something like a tambourine can become when you don't work with it on a regular basis. Rent or borrow any additional instruments in time to practice with them for a few days before the session. (I once worked with a band who figured they could pick up a few extra instruments in the studio and slap on some nice parts. These included tubular bells, vibes, sitar, cello and flute. You can't imagine how badly that session went.)

Make sure everyone is in good health and in a good state of mind about the studio. The more you think about what you're doing, the better prepared you're going to be. Most people blow the simple things because they're too busy worrying about the things they have no control over. So, on the day of the session, they realize that the piano is out of tune and they have barbed-wire for guitar strings. Wonderful. Little things like that make for crazy last minute pressures that start a session off with anxiety instead of confidence.

An artist must understand all the principals that go into a recording session. The engineer, the studio, the producer, the tunes, the arrangements, the players, the instruments, the vocal parts, the overdubs, and all the rest must be together. All of this is important for a demo and unquestionable for a master. The key is to prepare, but don't worry. Since that is pretty much impossible, don't start worrying about all the worrying you are doing. Don't psyche yourself out.

## Preparing The Tunes

Prepare three or four songs at a time and record them when you are ready. Nobody records an album in a week anymore (please don't write and tell us all the exceptions you know about —we don't care). A lot of artists make the mistake of working on ten songs at a time. By the time they have the tenth song down, they've forgotten the first. Even if you can learn all ten to the max, working on that many at once tends to blow the vibe. By doing four songs at a time, you always keep a fresh feeling about the material. Learn them, and when you're ready, record the basic track on all four (more about this later).

When preparing for the studio, try to peak the song in rehearsal without overdoing it. Once you are satisfied with your performance in every way, and you are able to perform it consistently at that level, then you are ready to record. Don't drive it into the ground and don't make changes just for the sake of making changes. If you are constantly changing a song every time you play it, you will never be able to bring it to its peak. You have to settle on the arrangement at some point, so that you can concentrate on learning it. Once you have been able to perform the song the way that you want it for three or four consecutive rehearsals, you are as ready as you will ever be to record.

Remember that your feeling about a performance can change. Don't be surprised if you listen to a tune that you tracked last week and realize that you could make a little change for the better. Once a song is recorded you shouldn't make a lot of changes, but if it's something you feel strongly about, give it a try. Don't spend a lot of time on it and if it's not working, just be satisfied with what you've got.

## Studio Musicians

Some of the greatest live players tend to freeze in the studio. They may be great on stage, but freak when they hear it come back over those big studio monitors. If you know you have a band member who might lose it in the studio, don't take any chances—get a pro. You're making a record that you will have to listen to for the rest of your life, so make it as good as possible. If your drummer's time is bad in rehearsal, it will probably be worse in the studio. He has to be willing to put his ego aside for the good of the record. Some of the greatest and most popular groups in the world have never used all their players on record. It may not be that they are not capable musicians. They can be fantastic players and still turn to bananas in the studio.

Using a session player to replace a band member does not have to be a permanent change. Perhaps things will be different by the next album. Ringo Starr did not play on the Beatles first single because it was decided that the session drummer did a better job, but his career certainly did not suffer because he was absent from "Love Me Do." The person who freezes in the studio can overcome his problem by playing on a lot of demo sessions to get used to the studio. But don't let him learn at the expense of your first record.

You may want to bring in a session player to add to your sound. Strings, horns, and even your basic track instruments can benefit from a good player's expertise. If bringing in the hottest guitar player in Nashville will make your band sound like the hottest new act in America, do it! Who cares about your ego? Are you in this for ego or to make the best record possible? (Besides, when your record hits Number One you can ego your brains out if you want to, but I hope you don't want to.)

Session players are paid union scale for the making of master recordings. The current rate is $137 for a three hour session, which is the minimum time you must purchase. There are some players who are getting double and triple scale, and the super players, like guitarists Lee Ritenour and Larry Carlton, may not play for less than a thousand a day.

## Being A Session Player

To be a session player, you must first master your instrument to the point where you can play almost anything on it. It is your job to play what someone wants you to play, and if you can't do it, you won't be called back. You should also learn to read music very well because session players are usually given a chart to follow. You may not have to play exactly what is on the chart, but you'd better be able to follow it well enough to ad lib in synch with everyone else.

To tell you how session players usually get started, I would like to introduce you to "Kid Fuzz." Kid Fuzz was six when he got his first guitar and played his first sock hop at thirteen. By the time he was eighteen, he had been in forty-three rock groups and decided that he would never be able to get along with anybody under those conditions. Besides, he didn't want to be a star. He just wanted to play his guitar. In fact, that was all he ever wanted to do. He tried playing solo gigs at various lounges, but since his voice was rather birdlike and nobody enjoyed dancing to thirty minute guitar solos, he gave it up. At nineteen, he knew his niche in life and struck out for L.A. to be a session guitarist.

Session players usually get started by hanging around the

studios and doing demos for everybody and their little brother. Kid Fuzz went to fourteen jam sessions before he even got to take his guitar out of his case, and then he broke a string. Finally he got a job laying carpet in a four track studio in the Valley. One day when he was doing the bathroom (studios are big on carpeting. They even carpet the walls and ceilings. Sometimes they even carpet their driveway) a local teenage rock group called "The Nasty" showed up to do their demo. The only problem was that "The Nasty's" lead player had broken his thumb drinking a bottle of beer the night before (don't ask how; these punk bands get hurt on every gig or else they consider it a bad night). Needless to say, the "Fuzz" filled in and the rest is history.

Well, not quite, but he did get another gig playing on a demo for "Johnny & The Wimps." The word was getting out that the Kid was a pretty hot player. A few established players were becoming familiar with his work. One day, when a semi-important rock group was getting ready to do their album, the Kid got a call. It seems that the group's regular guitar player got run over by an egg truck on the way to the studio, and the drummer suggested our man Fuzz. Before you could say wah-wah, the Kid was plugged in and ready to go. It went very well. The next week the horn player on the session is asked to produce an album and he calls Kid Fuzz. After about three months of steady gigs, one of the records that features Fuzz pops as a hit. The Kid's sound begins to be in demand. He is on call all the time and begins to do double and triple dates (two and three sessions in the same day).

The Kid becomes more choosey. On some dates he is promised leader fee. That means he gets double the rate and is responsible for directing the band in the studio (not with a baton). He makes suggestions and keeps everybody off of each others toes. After another year, four of the albums that feature the Kid on guitar turn platinum. He is now a star. Very few people outside of the music business recognize his name, but he is a star all the same. He earns in excess of $250,000 a year and could make more if he wanted to work harder. Every major artist has asked him to play on their album and seven record labels have offered him his own deal. He's not interested. He just likes to play guitar.

Exposure is the name of the game if you want to be a studio musician. Get in on as many sessions and meet as many players as possible. Be willing to jam with *anybody* and sooner or later the word will get out. You don't have to be Mister Personality, but you need to get along well with people. A lot of producers and artists choose their session players from various cliques of musicians who are close friends, but you don't have to be buddy-buddy to get a gig. You just have to be undeniably good.

A good session player must be able to respond well to instructions. Artists and producers are not the most articulate people when it comes to explaining nebulous things like a "raunchy," "red," "fat," "slick" or "electric-electric" guitar sound. You aren't expected to read minds, but you are expected to have patience and enjoy communication. Studio players should also not be afraid to make suggestions about what they play. You should feel free to throw out your ideas for consideration, but you must also know that when a decision has been made, it is time to shut-up. Some producers have definite ideas and don't like to have them second guessed. A good session musician will learn to deal positively with a variety of people in a variety of situations.

Lee Ritenour is one of the best known session guitarists in the business, and he describes the kind of versatility that is sometimes necessary. "I remember one day in particular, because each session was so radically different. In the morning I did a legit orchestra date. It was with a conductor and about a hundred musicians. At two o'clock I went down to Steve Cropper's studio and played on Keith Moon's record, and that was outrageous. That lasted until ten o'clock. After that I did an overdub for the Jackson's and they wanted a banjo part. It was a real mind-blower of a day."*

Ritenour's advice to beginning session players: "Getting along with people is probably a key, because I've seen some pretty great musicians who don't make it at anything they do because

---

* *Rock-Pop 11/10/78*

they're uptight. When you first start out, you're usually there because one of the guys on the tape recommended you when their regular favorite couldn't be there. At that point they're just happy if you can make the music sound right. The next step is that they call on you regularly, but they're asking you to sound like other people. Finally what happens is they're calling on you to sound like you, which is always the best thing.''*

A session player also has to be responsible and have a professional attitude. If the session is for six, don't show up at seven. You're responsible for your equipment, and that includes any funky gadgets that you like to use. You have to be organized because you are a businessman. You book your own dates, and run your own business.

The most important thing necessary to being a good session player is to play like crazy. Learn every technique you can, and practice, practice, practice. Magazines like "Guitar Player" and "Contemporary Keyboard" can greatly assist you in learning your craft. You are trying to become a master of a specific instrument and you want to learn everything you can about it.

## The Budget

The first thing to keep aware of in handling an album budget is keeping aware. You're not an accountant, but it certainly doesn't hurt to ask what you're spending. The worst place in the world to be is when you're going to put down the final vocal on the best song of the album and you find out that you're out of money. You've got to plan out your buget and keep track of what you are spending. Be sure to allow time for screw-ups. Otherwise you'll wind up scratching the horns, strings, and background vocals from the album to make up for the money you lost when your bass player couldn't find his bass (turned out that it was right where he left it—on the roof of the studio). Get your actual costs together and figure them out to the nearest dollar. Know where you can and can't cut costs. Know the prices of everything involved.

* Rock-Pop 11/10/78

## Prices

A typical first album budget for a self-contained band is forty to sixty thousand dollars. The record label may only put up enough money for four cuts, or maybe just enough for a single. Four tunes would probably be budgeted at around $20,000, depending on the label (which means it could be fifty bucks). Most of these worries are handled by the producer, but it is good to familiarize yourself with the various expenses that go into making a record.

Studio costs have been outlined in another chapter, but remember to shop around. Record labels usually won't try to stuff you into their own studio because they're aware that how an artist feels about the studio is more important than their making a few extra bucks on the deal. If you are faced with that situation and you know of a better studio with a smaller fee, don't be afraid to say no. You want to go where you feel comfortable and, after all, you are the one paying for the studio. The label will advance you money for recording costs, but it will be deducted from your royalties before you see a penny.

Another big expense is session musicians. If you're a self-contained band you might not use too many, unless you get into strings and horns. A string date with just twelve players will cost you two thousand dollars plus the cost of each chart, which could be anywhere from $150 to $500 each, depending on who is arranging it. If you want a fragile string sound, you may only want to use six or eight players, but if you want a nice, fat, and juicy sound, you might need eighteen or twenty-four strings. Since you are paying for three hours minimum time, you want to do all your string parts on the same day. (In a three hour string date you can do up to three or four songs.)

A string player is a string player, so don't be paying double or triple scale unless you're getting Zubin Metha. With strings, you need quantity. You will usually want ten or twelve guys, and you may want more. If you want the sound of the London Philharmonic, you can get it, but it will take at least eighteen players doubling their parts.

String players also have to be good. One or two bad players

in a string section will foul up the harmonies something awful. That's where the contractor does his job. The leader, or contractor, is paid double, and one of his jobs is lining up the best players he can get for the money. Hiring a high school player for $10 a tune is nice, but it will probably take you three hours to get the song down right. I would rather get the pro who can whip out a chart the moment you put it in front of him. You don't have rehearsal time for these guys. They've been trained all their life and they're expected to be able to play the chart perfectly after only a one-time run through.

With a self-contained band, the arrangements are usually done by the band and their producer, but in some cases it's a good idea to hire a professional arranger. With a string section, the person who does the arrangements will usually conduct as well. The conductor is paid double scale but his fee for arranging can vary considerably. The cheapest you can get a good arranger to work for is usually about $150 per tune. It is important to have charts for all your session players. A chart is like a road map, so it's a good idea to have one even if you have some idea of where you're going. Since you're paying a session musician to give his best performance, you should supply him with every possible tool that can help him.

By the way, make sure you use your sessions players wisely. Don't waste their talent because it's expensive. You have to be organized enough to make sure that you're ready for the player the moment he walks into the studio. Note: Don't use a triple scale guitar player for a simple basic track. You need these guys for the icing, because that's what they do best.

Another expense on a session is taxes. This is often a sweet surprise for a new artist. You have to pay taxes on all the talent fees that you pay. This includes singers, arrangers, musicians, jugglers, lion tamers, pole vaulters, and anybody else who has a union. The only people you don't pay taxes on are your producer, engineer, and the other members of your group, because these people aren't working out of a union. The taxes run around 20 to 25% of the fees and you pay them to Aftra (singers) or the American Federation of Musicians (musicians).

See how crazy it gets? In the beginning there is a tendency to only see that fat $60,000 budget and not all the piddly junk that eats it up. The budget must cover everything—producer's fees, the engineer's fees, tape costs, cassette copies, and the pizza you send out for at midnight.

## The 24-Track Monster

Now that you're all set to record, it's time to bring that horendous display of equipment facing you into its proper perspective. While it looks ominous, it's not really that big a deal once you understand it. Think of a 24 Track recorder as twenty four little mono machines all hooked together. It's just like the back room of the local Playback store except somebody snuck in and wired everything together. Through the modern wizzardry of electronics, there exists one machine that combines the functions of 24 little ones.

The 24 Track Studio only became the standard of the industry rather recently. At one time everything was recorded mono and then they developed two track. Then four track took the industry by storm, followed by eight track and sixteen track. The 16 Track studio didn't last long as the industry standard before the twenty-fours came in. (No, I don't know why they didn't continue multiplying by two, and go to 32 Track.) The value of having 24 Tracks can be summed up rather crudely in one word —isolation. Note: I am sure there are three-hundred-and-forty-seven points that I am overlooking from an electronic standpoint, but I am speaking as a producer. If you disagree, write me the most technical letter possible explaining why, because that way I won't have to read it since I won't understand it.

## Isolation

Isolation means being able to change a bass part fifteen times without screwing anything else up. Multitrack recording allows you to (in theory) record everything separately, which gives you a lot more ways to play with the sound. In order to make use of this wonderful advantage, you must not allow the instruments to "bleed" onto each other's tracks. You don't have the freedom to redo a guitar part if it's all over the bass track as well. I will beat this into your head severely in the next chapter, so don't worry too much about it now.

A two inch tape is a warehouse of sound. You can store all kinds of sounds in all kinds of places and then recombine them in totally different ways, if you so desire. Let's say you run out of tracks, but you've got to do some percussion in the chorus. You look over your track sheet and find that one of the guitars isn't doing anything in the chorus, so you store the percussion there until the mix. Obviously this can get very complicated, so it's important to keep precise notes of what's on the tracks. You also have to learn to keep your unused tracks clean because you might want to use them. That means that you shouldn't have talking, laughing, feet shuffling, belching, and all the like on the tape, because it will make more work to erase it later.

Remember that a great machine is nothing in the hands of someone who doesn't know how to use it. The most sophisticated studio in the world will sound like Tommy Tucker's Two Track if the wrong man is behind the controls.

Before you record, you should spend some time familiarizing yourself with studio procedure. Sitting in on a friend's session can be a great help and if you're going in for the first time, make sure that you do this. It's no big deal. The 24-Track Monster is just a tool and now it's your turn to use it.

# Chapter 8
# Recording Your Sound

*"When I was first starting out, I can remember going to the Sinatra sessions and they would be recording something like thirty-five instruments on a four track machine. It was amazing.*

**—Ted Templeman** *

While some of the topics discussed in this chapter apply to both demo and master recording, the focus is on work that is done for release as a record. Demo recording is covered in Chapter 5.

It is important that you realize the difference between recording and live performance. Recording is a new ballgame with different rules and different winners. You are now competing with artists who are well versed in the science of modern recording. They know how to make all that junk work for them, so you'd better know it too. And don't let the engineer hear you refer to electronic wizzardry as "junk" either. You need the engineer because he's the one who knows how to help you

* © *Musician's Guide (Ted Templeman: Artistry In Sound by James Riordan 2/78)*

avoid all the pitfalls of recording. Along with your producer, he can help you turn that exciting live sound into an exciting record.

Also , don't get carried away with trying to get a "live" sound on tape. If you want the record to sound "live," record it live. Some artists use the phrase "live sound" to mean an energetic sound with a lot of feeling. You *can* get that on record by using the studio in the way it was meant to be used. In fact, that is what you are trying to achieve.

## Studio Moxy

Studio Moxy can be learned the hard way by years of experience in the studio. Every time you make a costly mistake or blow a session, remember what you did wrong, and after a few years you will have a good knowledge of studio moxy. An easier way is to watch *other* people make mistakes and blow sessions and learn from what *they* did wrong. This is less painful. In fact, if you're rather a mean sort, it can even be a lot of fun. Seriously folks, do some serious hanging around at recording sessions. Pay attention and you can learn a lot. Also, talk to as many people in the field as you can. Ask them about practical things rather than technical ones. Musicians shouldn't have to deal with how many tootches are going into the kanutian valve and how far you have to open a kanutian valve before you have a rebe-strebbe. Engineers have to deal with that stuff (engineers even *like* to deal with that stuff). You want to know what makes a session go smoothly and what tends to screw it up. The best way to learn those things is by watching them happen, but to start you off, I've compiled some tips, based on *my* mistakes.

Start with an easy song. Begin recording with a tune that everyone like to play, because that should get the adrenaline going. If you have a song that everyone feels will be a smash, it may be good to start with that one. It's smart to go for the hits quick, because it really psyches you up to hear them playing back. It's the old carrot in front of the nose trick. Some songs are so good they even smell like money (not to me, of course, because I'm an *artist* and money is only a secondary thing, but there are those who are more crass in their values . . . ha, ha).

Whatever song you start with, don't beat it into the ground. If it's not happening, take a break and move on to something else. I remember beginning this one session with the song that the band always did right. It was by far the easiest, and they could play it flawlessly in their sleep. In their sleep maybe, but not in the studio on that day. Twenty-four takes later, I decided to try another tune. A good decision, but made a little too late to save that day's work. By that time the band was scared to death. If, after twenty-four takes, they still couldn't get their *easiest* song down, what was going to happen with the hard ones? It was my mistake. I should have recognized that, for some reason, the song was becoming a stumbling block and, after three or four takes, moved on to something else. Sometimes a band will make careless mistakes which will stop after a few takes. Other times the mistakes become psychological and the only way to overcome them is by coming back to the song at a later time. It is a producer's job to know the difference, but after twenty takes, he should have a clue.

A good headphone mix is tantamount to good recording. If the musicians aren't hearing themselves correctly, they are not going to play correctly. There are a lot of things the engineer does before the tape begins to roll that are very important to the success of the session, but the headphone mix also depends on the musicians to some extent. They have to *tell* him what they need to hear in the phones. I've seen some sessions where the musicians were so intimidated that they didn't want to keep "hassling" the engineer with remixing their headphones. That's stupid. Getting that headphone mix the way you want it is part of his job, and without it you can't do yours.

Another good point is not wasting a lot of time listening to playbacks. Don't stop after each take, take off the instruments, rewind the tape, and trudge into the control room to listen to the playback. Remember that it takes as long to listen as it does to record, so put a few tracks down and *then* listen. Do one take and listen to it, but after that do three or four takes at a time. Don't stop unless everybody *knows* they've got it. Stopping and listening just to hear the bass player say, "Yeah, that's where I thought I blew it" is crazy. You also don't need to continue through a song if somebody screws up. You can do a lot of things to repair a mistake, but most of the time it's just better to do another take.

The simplest axiom to remember is *"when the red light is on, you're working."* When the recording light isn't on, you're just spending money. You're there to record and the more time you actually spend getting something down on tape, the better off you will be.

Of course, all the studio moxy in the world won't help if the vibrations are bad. If the artist feels intimidated by the producer or the engineer, he won't be able to give his best—especially if he feels that his best won't be good enough for the producer anyway, or if his best will be lost because of the producer's lack of ability. If the artist hears a playback and doesn't like the sound of his voice or his guitar, he should say what he feels, because unless that is changed, the vibe will be lost. In fact, preserving the vibe in the studio is so important, the next section is devoted to it.

## Staying Hot & Not Blowing The Vibe

It's real easy to blow the vibe in a recording session. No matter how slow you try to take things, there is still going to be a certain amount of pressure. Egos are going to flare up and everyone is more sensitive to criticism. It's important, therefore, for everybody to realize that they have to maintain their cool. Don't be snappy with each other. Be even more polite in the studio than you are out of it, because everyone's nerves are on edge. In practice, you might be able to tell your drummer that his time stunk on that last tune, but you'd better be more tactful in the studio. When artists are recording, they are engaged in a creative process, an art form, so understandably their sensitivity will be increased (this' means both kinds of sensitivity— the flower smelling kind and the pissed-off kind).

The key to staying hot is not blowing the vibe. When everyone in the studio is encouraging and positive about what is happening, the quality of work is also on a much higher level. The more relaxing the atmosphere, the less pressure and, in most cases, the better the results.

It is also important to take advantage of a "hot streak" in the studio. When everyone feels good and is performing well, do as much as possible. If you've still got some time left after finishing what you were planning on doing that day, go for some more. By the same token, when you feel you're real close to getting a particular track down, that is not the time to take a cigarette break. When it feels good to play, keep on playing!

The opposite is also true. When you're cold, tense, and everything you play sounds like oatmeal mush—go home! Just call it a day. When you make your deal with the studio, you should ask them if you will be billed for time that you don't use. If you get done early on a particular day or if everything falls apart and you call the session early, you shouldn't have to pay for the full time. Most studios understand these things and won't charge you, because you're doing your whole project there anyway and they want to treat you right. But you should still ask. Say something like, "will we be billed for any time that we don't use, and if we will, I don't want to record here." Another function of your producer is to recognize when everybody's had it for the day and send them home. You can waste a lot of dough trying to record at one level when you feel at another (that doesn't mean you can go home every time you get a tummy ache either).

Note: Don't expect the studio to cut you a lot of slack in regard to your session ending on time. Not charging you for going home early is one thing, but letting you run overtime is another. If there's a string date with twenty people waiting outside the studio and you're messin' around with tape copies, you could lose friends fast. When someone else is scheduled to come in the studio after your session ends, then you'd better plan on ending at the right time.

Something which doesn't directly relate to staying hot or blowing the vibe, but which does affect both and can lead to a great amount of wasted time, is the making of tape copies. Believe it or not, everyone on the session and his dog does not need a tape copy. I've seen some sessions where all six band members, two of the session musicians, and the janitor wanted two tape copies each. And the janitor wanted an 8-track for his car as well. Seriously, you want as few tape copies as possible. Making a lot of tape copies costs money and time. If you need to analyze what's happening, get one copy and have everybody listen to it together. Don't make five different cassettes for everybody in the band. Usually the only constructive listening will occur when everyone is together anyway.

Wait for the finished product before you start playing it for your friends. Otherwise, you are opening the door for things which could affect your attitude in the studio. What happens is the bass player's best friend decides that "playing on the two and the four might work better here." So the next day the bass player freaks and calls everybody else in the band, saying he has to change his part. Before you know it, you've got a catastrophe over something that is basically garbage. Leave the opinions to the people who are part of the project. You agreed on them in the beginning and if you need an outside opinion before the final mix is done, there is some kind of a confidence problem. I don't like to play anything that is unfinished for anyone. Whenever you play something that is unfinished, you are depending upon the imagination of the listener to fill in the missing pieces. Very few people who are not directly involved with the project can do that. The only people who have a right to hear "works in progress" are the people who are making and paying for the record. Besides, tape copies are a pain for the producer (me).

## A Word About Drugs And Records

The word is caution. Invariably, the greatest enemy in a recording session is drugging out. Do enough drugs in a session and pretty soon everything will start to sound good. There is an infinitesimal number of things that you can do to a record. You can change and overdub to infinity if you want to, and sometimes when you're loaded, you want to do just that. You stop making a record and start playing with the board like it was an electronic computer basketball game. It all sounds great that night, but wait until you hear it the next morning. Talk about hangovers. Imagine a thousand dollar hangover! It may cost that much to correct what you did while being too loaded to care.

You have to be discerning when you're making a record. Some drugs give you a rush to create and an excitement about creativity. That can be great, but you have to realize that it is not real and drug highs are not captured on tape. It might sound good if your audience always listens to it as stoned as you were when you recorded it, but in that case, are you really producing art? If someone has to be zonked to like your music, you are really limiting your creative and commercial potential.

I don't want to give you the idea that everybody who makes records does drugs, but the two are frequent companions. Drugs in their proper perspective are your own business, but don't blow a career because you got so high in the studio you thought you were recording Sgt. Peppers, and the next day it came out like Phil & Zelda's Bowling Alley Band.

Drugs also have a tendency to slow up sessions in other ways. Everybody needs a joint break, or a coke break, or whatever. And during the break all these wonderful etherial ideas come out which really louse up the progress of the session. People start thinking of the weirdest things to do to their music. The problem is that most of the time they can't even explain them, much less perform them. They might start out okay, but before you know it, they want to record everything backwards or make funny noises into the mic. Drugs do have a way of bringing out our creative abilities, but they do so in a way which can really hinder our work. It's like a writer who, after getting loaded, has all these wonderful ideas, but when he sits down to type, all that comes out is numbers and question marks. 1??87*??3921?. His mind is functioning at a creative level, but his fingers can't perform the simplest functions. You have to perform functions in the studio which require precision and timing. And you have to be very objective and discerning about sound. Drugs and the studio can go together, but be very careful that you don't overdo it.

## The Basic Track: The Foundation For Your House

The basic track is the foundation of your record and you want it uncluttered and correct. Records today are made like skyscrapers, and in order for the twenty stories above the ground to keep standing, the four stories below the ground have to be solid foundation. The basic track is the first thing you record and it has to "hold" the rest of your record all the way through the layering process.

Basics are primarily concerned with rhythm and groove, because it is these two elements which make up the "feel" of a record. The basic track is usually composed of the bass, drums, and one or two other instruments playing a rhythm part (like guitars or keyboards). The drums and bass are usually laying the groove (pocket, foundation, danceability, schwartz, Memphis Bite, or pink bagel), and the other instruments are playing a rhythm pattern in and around this pulse.

Another reason the basic track is so important is that it is made up of things you can't repair. You can change everything else, but you can't change that basic track. The bass and the drums have got to lock into the right feel, in order for anything else to come out right. If the bass and the drums are fighting each other, you've got problems. Of course, you need to have all of this worked out, and that "feeling" recognized and locked-in, before you go near a studio.

You must be concerned about leakage when recording basic tracks. This is true even if you aren't recording in California during the rainy season. No, what I'm talking about is *sound leakage*. Remember, I told you that *isolation* was very important in 24-Track recording (or in any multi-track recording). One reason is that the more isolated an instrument is, the less it will leak onto the tracks that belong to other instruments. The more leakage you have, the less freedom you have. Overdubs don't usually have a leakage problem because they are most often recorded one instrument at a time. Since basic tracks are composed of a group of instruments being recorded at the same time, there is more danger of leakage. Baffles and positioning in the studio help immensely, but the louder you play, the more leakage you are going to get (by the way, baffles are those huge overstuffed pillows that you keep walking into when you first visit a studio. They are there to absorb sound, which they do even better than they absorb your face when you run into them).

I know that if you are one of these guys who has every knob on his amplifier glued at "10" this is going to hurt your feelings, but there isn't too much I can do about it. You simply can't play at screaming volumes on a basic track. For one thing, you are using five hundred and thousand dollar microphones in the studio, and that means *you don't have to play loud.* There is no reason to play loud on a basic track. The mics are going to pick you up and the board can raise the volume as much as you want in the mix. The only other reason you would have for playing loud would be to get distortion, and you don't need distortion on a basic track. Save the volume for the overdubs where it matters and doesn't get in the way of everything else.

Let's say you get all the way through a ten minute song and the bass player misses a note. If there's no leakage, that's no big deal. You just punch him in and correct the flub. But if he's all over the guitar, keyboard, and drum tracks, you may not be able to repair the mistake without making them redo their parts as well. You will have to leave the bad note on their tracks or else record the whole thing over because you won't be able to punch-in everybody ("punching-in" is going from playback to record in time to correct a mistake in a track without erasing any other part of it. To be able to do it, you must have half a beat of rest between notes. "Punching-out," on the other hand, requires half a beat of unrest between the eyes before the other person can smack you back).

You can retrack the bass and the rhythm parts if you've got a good drum track and *no* leakage. It is even easier if the bass is going direct into the board and not through a mic. It is, however, almost impossible to retrack the drums. I have seen it done, but most people shudder at the thought of trying to retrack the drums and make them fit with the rest of the instruments that are already on tape. You're better off re-recording the whole song.

You must make sure that the tempo is right. If it's speeding up or slowing down, the groove is going to be lost and the feel is going to drive the listener away from the song, rather than lock him into it. If you have tempo problems, use a digital metronome. Known in the studio vernacular as a "click track," it can be sent through the headphones to all the tracking musicians. Since the drummer and the bass player should be playing "to" each other anyway, there is nothing wrong with using a click track to keep them together.

Many records begin with just the bass and drums laying down the basic track. Then the rhythm instruments do their thing and the layering process begins. In an effort to minimize leakage, I've heard of bands beginning with just the drums. As I've indicated, this can be very difficult, but if the drummer knows the song well, you can run a rhythm machine on one track and let him play to it. When he's done, the bass player will go in and lay down his part. I've also seen a basic done with five pieces at once, but everything is very isolated. It really depends upon the players and the amount of isolation the studio can offer. If you're using professional session players and you've got three hours to cut two or three songs, you should have no problem. Most of these guys play so many sessions that their time is perfect. The less experience you have, however, the more isolation you need.

## Less Is More

Assuming that you are not a seasoned pro, it is better to do your foundation with as few instruments as possible (by the way, it takes more to be a seasoned pro than completing all 347 of the Mel Bay Guitar Instruction Booklets . . . it takes experience as well). Make sure that everything is *isolated*. You don't need fifteen Marshall amps to do a rhythm guitar part, but if you "have to have" them, make sure you are isolated by overdubbing your part. The more isolation you can create, the easier it will be for you farther down the road. It gives you a cleaner sound, saves you a lot of studio time, makes your engineer happy, and most importantly, it gives you the freedom you need to experiment and make the best record possible.

It's very sad when you go to change a bad rhythm part and realize that you can hear it on the drum track. This usually happens when the drummer has cut the greatest track of his career. All because your amp was turned up too loud (the drummer will hate you forever). Listen to your engineer when he tells you to turn down. Making sure things are isolated is to *your* benefit. Less is more.

## Singing With The Track

Sometimes the singer has to sing along while the basic is being recorded in order to give the players the right feeling. This takes a little more work to set up, but if it helps get that basic track right, it's worth it. This is just a working vocal which can later be replaced by a more polished one. While the vocal is not the important thing at this step, you want to make sure that it gets recorded. Sometimes it turns out to be a great performance which the singer is not ever able to recapture. Of course, you must be sure that the singer is in an isolation booth so that he doesn't "bleed" onto everybody else's track. Work vocals are also good because a lot of singers do better when they're recording with the band. It gives them the feel of a live performance and that special thing of playing together. So remember to record these vocals and don't erase them until you have something better.

## Tracking

There are a few variances on how to track a session. I use five tracks for the drums, but some producers only use four. I like to use one track for the kick drum, one for the snare, one for the hi-hat, and two overheads (one on each side). The engineer may have to use ten mics to get those five tracks of sound into the board. On the bass, you should only use two tracks at the max. One should be direct into the board and one should be miked live (one more time: make sure the bass isn't loud enough to "leak" into something else). Most of the other basic track instruments will just require one track.

Often artists become impatient with the basic tracks because they want to get to the overdubs where they can be more "creative." That would be like God creating man before he had an earth to put him on. The best overdubs will sound stinko on a bad basic track. The basic has to be right. When they poured the foundation for your house it didn't look like much, but it was enough to hold the house. The basic may not sound like much to you, but it better be strong enough to hold the rest of your record. If it's not, it will all come tumbling down, and that includes you.

## Overdubs & Vocals

After you record your basic tracks, you are ready to overdub. It is much easier to do the basics for all the tunes you are planning on recording before you go on to the overdubs. The reason is that all your basics will have much the same instrumentation and are therefore miked the same way. This is another reason you should only concentrate on three or four tunes at a time.

The order I use for overdubbing is normally work vocal, background vocals, instrument solos, icing (horns, strings, chocolate frosting), final lead vocals, and extra percussion. This can vary a little depending on the tune and the act, but it's a good general guideline.

If you haven't already got a work vocal, you should put one on right after the basics are finished. Don't waste a lot of time with it because you'll recut it later. Its purpose is for a point of reference so that you will be sure to leave enough room for the final vocal as you do the rest of your overdubbing. Next, you should put on the background vocals for the same reason. At this point you should be able to clearly hear what holes you have to fill without stepping on the vocals. Now, do your instrument solos, like the guitar break or synthesizer solo, or whatever. After this, if you need horns or strings, you can put them in the proper perspective. Remember to do all the songs that require strings on the same day so that you can save on musicians' fees. You've got to pay these guys for three hours, so you might as well use the time. This means that, before the orchestra is called in, you have all the songs you're going to use them on developed to the point we've discussed. The basics, work vocal, background vocals, and solos are already done.

The final vocal should be cut after all the instrumental parts, with the possible exception of percussion. Remember to save the work vocal because you don't know you can top it until you do. When you get a lead vocal you're satisfied with, you can decide whether you want to add some percussion. Of course, if you're doing an instrumental record, the lead instruments (the ones playing the melody line or hooks) should be recorded after the basic track so that you don't cover them up with horns, strings, or whatever. Percussion should usually be done last unless you are doing a latin type of record or anything where the percussion is very vital to the feel.

When recording vocals, make sure that you like the sound of your voice in the headphones and that you feel comfortable with the volume of the music. *Communicate* with the engineer. Try to relax and get into the song. It's better to miss a few notes and get the feeling right. If you have an urge to sing something a little differently than you usually do it, give it a try. There are things that happen in the studio that don't occur anywhere else. Maybe you've never tried to hit a high "C" note in this one spot, but you've got a feeling you could do it now. Go for it! You never know until you try, and the studio can produce superhuman efforts sometimes. Also, remember that it will never be perfect, and very few singers are ever satisfied with their performance. Trust your producer and realize when you need to accept what you have, instead of going for more.

## The $250,000 Toy

The biggest problem I've encountered in doing overdubs is that people never know when to stop. They get so enthralled with having 24 tracks to play with that they think they have to use them all. You will always be able to hear something else to add. The question is not knowing what to put on next, but when to stop. Don't overproduce. I've ruined a lot of records because I thought they needed horns and strings. Many times it is better to go with the basic track, a few guitar licks, some handclaps, and the vocals. If you've got a great feeling in a song and the vocalist gave one hell of a performance, you don't need much more. You don't have to use all those tracks.

Twenty-four tracks are the standard of the industry. That means it is used for symphony orchestras and large choirs as well as a four piece band. So, don't feel guilty about open tracks. Leaving some tracks open is always a good idea. It allows you to do mini-mixes which can make the overall mix much easier. A good engineer can mix down the drums, bass, and rhythm instruments to three or four tracks. The result is that when you do the final mix, you only have to deal with eight or nine pots instead of twenty. Leaving some tracks open also allows the producer and the engineer to put in some good effects which can really improve the sound.

If you are being conservative in your production and you find that you still need *more* tracks, there are some things you can do. For example, you can do a mini-mix on your four drum tracks down to one or two tracks, and thereby free two more tracks to record. This is called ping-ponging, and it means to move tracks together (for example: the ping from Track 7 is ponged to Track 10).

## The Mix

The mix is where the producer's work really begins. This is where you blend all the recorded sounds together. If you're making a cake, you can have all the right ingredients, but if you fail to blend them according to the recipe, it could still come out tasting like a mud pie. It's the same with sound.

There are an infinite number of ways that you can combine the sounds that go into making a record. Besides determining the right volume for each sound, you can have some things heard on the right (speaker), some to the left, and some in the "center (both speakers). This is called "panning." You can have the drums to both the extreme right and left, the guitar overdub more in the "middle," the vocals on the left, the rhythm instruments on the right, and the synthesizer shifting from the left to the right, and back again. You can also change the specific sounds you have recorded by a variety of ways, which includes things like slap-echo, digital delay, equalization, and a lot of others.

The mix is also the place where the producer can pull out a lot of things he doesn't want to use. It's like when they make a movie they shoot way more film than they intend to use. In the mix the producer can blend, change, subtract, and add sound. The mix is the difference between a record and a whole bunch of sounds.

It is the producer's job to do the mix, and generally the fewer people who "help" him, the better. He may allow a few band members to be present, but he's crazy if he allows all of them to be there at the same time. Sometimes it is good to have a second opinion, but nobody needs fourteen different opinions. In most cases, the drummer would like to hear a little more drums, the guitarist would prefer the volume was upped on the guitar, the bass player believes his instrument should be raised on the mix, and so on. Producers who play a specific instrument even have to watch out that they don't raise the volume of that instrument in the mix, because they have a tendency to favor it.

When I'm ready to mix, I make copies with everything equal in volume on all 24 tracks, so that I don't miss anything. I don't want any surprises. By the time I'm ready to mix, I usually know what I want to hear, but I still take the tape home and listen to it. I try to make a few notes and preplan the mix before we begin. It's better to listen at home than to pay a studio $150 an hour for that privilege.

A lot of times when you actually start mixing, you will find that some of the things you wanted to do won't work, so you have to be prepared to make adjustments. It really helps to know what you want in the mix, but there is still a lot of experimenting involved.

Computerized mixing is a real benefit to mixing the sound levels. A computer won't get the sound you want, but it will remember what volume you chose to hear it. Once you go through and decide the volume level, you just punch-in the computer and it will remember those levels for you. This is very time saving because there is an incredible number of subtle volume changes in a mix. Without the computer, you have to remember them all, each time you mix. If you decided you wanted to raise the volume of the background vocals on the vamp, you have to do everything over, and if you forgot to fade the crash cymbol at this one point, you have to do it all again. The computer mixers they have today can even upgrade what you have on the data track without changing anything else. A producer used to need to have ten hands. Now he only has to have four.

Never rush through a mix. It has to be right, so take your time. Realize that mixing is the final stage of the studio process, and there are an infinite number of ways that you can do it, including some that would blow all the work that has already been done. On the other hand, you can second guess yourself to death. If it sounds good to you, the levels are right, the effects are there, there's not too much, and most importantly, you feel good about it, then roll it!

## Picking A Single

In most cases this is done by the record company, based on the response they get from radio programmers to specific cuts on the album. When you're starting out, you don't want to go against what the promotion people decide, because if they don't like the song, they won't promote it. If it's your first album and you feel in your gut that it should be one certain song, but the label's promo people feel it should be another, there isn't much you can do. There will come a time in your career when what you say here matters more than the opinions of others, and when that time comes, you have to recognize it, but that may never happen if you alienate the people who are responsible for making your record a hit. Your clout determines whether your choice is accepted.

There are also electronic testings that measure the response in a random subject when they hear a particular record. Many record labels employ these services and they can be very accurate, but sometimes they are way off base. Part of the problem is that they measure what the public likes, which is not always what the radio stations will allow them to hear. I don't mean to infer that a radio programmer is not human (some artists would argue this point), but when it comes to listening to records, he is not part of the general public either. He is a professional listener and he is the man who has to like your single. The best method of picking a single is to send out an entire album and see what cuts the stations start playing. I like to go with the song that grabs me the most and gets other people (like the label) the most excited, but it is the radio stations which are the deciding factor (more on this later).

## Mastering: Turning Cold Tapes Into Hot Records

Mastering is an art unto itself. This is where you take the tape that you've mixed and turn it into a record. It is done by using a mastering lathe and electronically cutting the sound (the groove) onto a master acetate. This is plated, and parts and stampers are made to press the records.

A lot of records are blown in the mastering process. You're going from tape to disc and it is very critical. You need to have a good mastering room and a good mastering engineer. It's not hard to find them and see what they have done. Usually their walls are also chock full of gold discs commemorating all the tapes they've turned into hot records (everybody has gold records on their wall in this business). Good mastering engineers deserve their gold records because it is a crucial factor in the success of a record.

It's very possible to make a record sound as good as a tape, but ninety-nine percent of today's recording artists do not realize what is involved. Ask one how many grooves a record has and you'll get all kinds of neat answers. A record only has one continuous groove. The amount of sound and the degree of volume is governed by the depth and width of that groove. The deeper the groove, the wider it must be. The wider it is, the less time there is available on the side. If there is a long amount of time on the side, the groove can't be deep and wide. If you try to put a lot of volume (a deep and wide groove) in a lengthy song, the grooves will kiss and you get skips. That's why record labels and radio stations always want short singles. A short single can be cut at a much louder volume than a long one, and this enables it to "jump" out at you from the radio or at least not be lower in volume than the records it is competing with.

It may be very artistic to have 24 minutes a side on your

album, but your record will never sound as good as your tape. You can argue that the Beatles pulled it off with the White Album and Sgt. Peppers, but these records were recorded in a way to not have a lot of bass bottom on the songs. If the bass and drums are pumping on all five or six songs on the side, they will have to be short numbers or else they won't sound good. If you want to have a lot of bass and drums in your music, keep your sides short or you will lose some of the brilliance.

The hotter the cutting needle, the deeper and wider the groove and the louder the sound. When someone refers to a record as being "cut hot" they mean that the sound is loud, so the cutting needle was probably very hot. Note: in most cases, the people who use this term will not be aware that they mean what they mean, so don't ask them about it or you will look like a dummy.

If your music is hard rock n' roll, you'd better keep the length down to 17 or 18 minutes per side. You're not cheating anybody because you want to give them the best sound you can. If you try to put 23 minutes of jamming bass, kicking drums, screaming vocals, and Jimmy Page guitar, the record will sound like it was made on a portable cassette player. Forty-fives often sound better than the same cut on an album because they are cut much hotter.

You can also do some editing in the mastering room. Editing is the art of moving dead weight, and while it is usually done in the mix, it can also be done by a good mastering engineer. In fact, these guys are some of the best editors in the world because they do it all the time. If you can edit out a particular section of a song and make the hook happen quicker, or the song move better, or get a "hotter" recording, do it!

After the master part is cut, it is plated. From this plate, stampers are made to press out the discs. Each stamper only lasts for a certain number of pressings, so they are continually replaced as more and more records are pressed.

Don't take mastering for granted. I've heard many artists claim that the records they got back couldn't have been cut from the tapes they turned in. If you leave it up to the record company, the first thing you might do after hearing the disc is vomit. A lot of groups just don't see it all the way through and they regret it. Fleetwood Mac is a powerful exception. They don't let anybody touch anything until the final disc is in their hands. And that care has paid off for them in sound quality.

The producer should be there when the record is mastered. He should also insist on a test record of the outcome. The producer knows how the record should sound. He was there from the day it was rehearsed to the day it became a disc. The sound can be blown anywhere in the creative process, so you have to pay attention all the way down the line. It's even possible to cut a great master and blow the test record. They might not have cut a good part from the master, or maybe they left it in the bath too long, or whatever. The important thing is to check it out step by step. Nobody can ever fault you for caring about your art, and if your name is going on it, you'd better make sure it is right.

# Chapter 9
# The Manager, Agent & Attorney

*"Personal management is a combination of two sides. One side is handling all of the artist's business, including his promotion and every day business. The other side is keeping the artist's creative perspective tuned in to what's going on in the real world."*

—**Irving Azoff** *

## Managers—What They Do

The prime reason you pay a manager anywhere from 10 to 50% of your earnings is that his knowledge and clout can make the difference between winding up a star and just winding up. He can get you where you want to go much faster than you can get there on your own. What might take you a year of hard hustling to complete could take him fifteen minutes and one phone call.

You're a business, and the function of a manager is to help you operate it. He is literally a partner in your career. Most people think that a manager works magic and some of them

* © *The Platinum Rainbow 1980.*

seem to do just that, but it's all based upon their knowledge of this business and the people they know in it. A manager knows that labels would be most interested in your act and how to approach them. He knows who is the best agent for you, the right publicist, and he can help you find a suitable attorney and accountant. He knows how to handle promoters who want to pay you zero against 50% of nothing. He'll help you put your road crew together, get equipment and transportation for the stage, and even take you shopping for the right stage clothes if you need him to. He represents you to everybody and he is a little of all things to you.

## Picking The Right One & When You Need One

You want a manger who has been around long enough to gain the knowledge and make the contacts. Someone who can get a record company executive on the phone when he needs to and someone who can afford to say no when the deal isn't right. A big time manager can get you a record deal, but a small timer can *keep* you from getting one. A manager without power is worthless.

In most cases your manager should be financially solvent. If he's busy looking for the bucks to pay his rent, he can't be spending as much time hustling your career. There are some guys who have clout and knowledge, but haven't found a way to make them pay off yet. They may be able to help your career because of their sincerity and belief in your talent, but you have to realize that if they really had it together they wouldn't be struggling. Another advantage of a big-time manager is that he can package you with some of the well known artists that he is handling. This can be very advantageous.

Unfortunately, the nature of the music business often requires a manager to be aggressive and even pushy. Consequently, you don't want someone whose primary qualification is that they are a nice person and people like them. People in this business will screw you over, whether they like you or not. You want someone who has a lot of guts and the power and energy to back it up. You do *not* want a yes-man. If you want someone to hold your hand and tell you how great you are, you can choose between your mother, Aunt Sara, your girl friend, or a house of ill repute. You don't want a namby-pamby relationship with your manager. You want a guy who is strong and forceful enough to kick you in the ass when you need it, but not when you don't.

As I mentioned in Chapter 2, record labels love to work with a group that has a good manager. They know that if they put up some money for promotion, he won't let it go to waste. They know he can do it right because he's already done it with other acts.

A lot of young artists make the mistake of getting a manager before they really need one. They just like the sound of saying things like "my Manager will call you." You don't need a manager to book your act into the Moonlight Skating Palace. When bands are first starting out, there always seems to be one close friend who can't play an instrument and he almost automatically becomes the group's manager. You know the guy. He sells men's clothing by day and manages bands by night. He couldn't book a Beatles reunion concert if he had their help. You don't need a manager until the rest of your act is really together, and that includes good original tunes and a solid stage show. The chances are that you won't be able to interest a good manager until you're at this point anyway (nice how that works out, isn't it?). You need a manager to get a label and prepare your act for a national tour, and until you're ready for those things, a manager would be wasting his valuable time. Get extensive playing and recording (demo) experience before you get a manager.

There's nothing wrong with having one of your friends help you get your pictures together and book gigs for you, as long as both of you understand that there will come a time in your career when you're going to be looking for a record deal and you will need someone else to help you find it. Firing your best friend can be a real hassle, but if you have a mutual understanding before you begin to work together, the problem is lessened considerably. He can still stay in the picture as your road manager or as an assistant to the bigtime manager that you need to get you over the hump.

Very rarely a friend-manager who started with the band is able to take them all the way. Invariably, when this occurs, the key to it is an unstoppable hit record. Remember, a hit song breaks all the rules. When the Doobie Brothers were first managed by Bruce Cohn, he was not a seasoned, experienced manager. He was just a friend of the band, but the record "Listen To The Music" was a guerrilla hit. The label jumped on it and now, years later, Bruce is a hell of a big-time manager. Of course, everyone likes to think that they have a song that is going to break down all the doors for them, but the reality is that you will probably have to go one step at a time. So when you're ready for it, the best policy is to obtain the best possible management.

Most big managers need a deadweight act like they need a hole in the thumb. A real heavy isn't going to take you on unless he intends to do something for you to make it worth his while. Anybody who falls all over themselves to work with you probably needs you more than you need them, which means you don't want them for your manager (see how skitzo it gets. The only guys you want are the guys who don't want you at first.) A big time manager has to be impressed. A small time manager tries to impress you.

When you walk into the guy's office and you see pictures of 43 different acts on the wall (with names like "Who Done It & The What Fours") and he wants to book you into Bushville, Maryand before he even sees your act, you might reconsider working with him. In fact you might consider running out of his office at breakneck speed. You want a guy who doesn't *need* you. If you know that his 20% out of your career isn't going to make or break him, you'll feel more secure in the relationship. You want a guy who is interested in you for the challenge and the big money rather than someone who is concerned with peanut dough. The guy in Bushville with the 43 pictures on his wall needs all 43 of those acts just to make his monthly nut. You don't want a guy who's sweating the thirty bucks a night he can make from your gig. You want someone who is building toward a commission of four grand a night. Someone who knows you might need six months to develop your act in the big time, but isn't worried because he is secure.

## Dealing With Managers

The way that your manager is paid, of course, depends on the arrangement you have with him. Some managers would prefer to collect the money for you and then subtract their percentage and forward the rest to you. Most good managers, however, wouldn't touch an artist's money with a twelve foot pole (everything is a little bigger in the music business). They know that if relations ever go bad, the ramifications of controlling the artist's money can go against them. Instead, the top managers try to set you up with a good business manager or accountant to handle your money. The manager might give you a list of these people to contact so you can pick out the one you like. Once you agree on a business manager or accountant, all of your monies will be paid to them and they will deduct your manager's fee and distribute the rest as you direct.

As far as percentages go, there is no set standard. Twenty percent is good. But it depends on what it's worth to you. I've heard of 50%! Would you rather get 50% of two million dollars a year, or 80% of two hundred thousand a year? If a really big name manager who handles (not *used* to handle) several top acts wants to work with you and charge you fifty percent, I think it would be worth it. On the other side of the coin, if you need money to develop your act, you should be able to ask your manager for an advance and expect to get it (you can't be preparing for the studio and working construction twelve hours a day unless you're planning on being a virtuoso on the saw and hammer). This is another advantage of getting a manager who is financially successful. You can't expect a struggling manager to free you from your day gig because he simply doesn't have the bread, but you should expect it from a guy who has hundred dollars bills falling out of his nose every hour or so. Don't be asking the guy to buy you a Rolls or anything stupid like that, but an advance which allows you to focus your energy more on your music, or buys you some new equipment, is a different story.

How long you sign with a manager can vary considerably. There are one and two year deals, three year deals, five year deals, and longer. Most contracts also have a series of options which are renewable at the manager's discretion. Sometimes these options will only take effect if the artist has earned a certain amount during the contract period. I have seen contracts with as many as four or five additional option periods of five years each. That's thirty years! You can't blame a manager for asking you to sign a five year deal, because he's going to be putting out a lot of time and money into your career and he wants to be there when the returns start coming in. The options should be based on a mutual decision, or have some sort of financial standard included, so that the artist isn't bound forever with no guaranteed financial gain.

Actually, most of the really big managers don't use contracts until they are really doing something for you. They don't throw a contract at you as soon as they see you. One reason is that they know that, in many ways, a contract is not worth the paper it is written on. If the two people involved don't get along, they will find a way to get out of the deal. A lot of new artists think that contracts are the end of the world. If you want out of a deal, just go to an attorney and refuse to pay your manager until you negotiate another deal. The manager can fight you in court and cause you a lot of grief, but he's tying up his time and money as well as yours. A good manager knows that you've got to trust him and he's got to trust you, in order for the relationship to work. And no contract in the world can secure that trust like good communication.

In fact, I know a lot of big-time managers who don't even bother with contracts. They have a gentlemen's agreement. If the artist stiffs them, they stop working for him. It's very simple and it saves a lot of lawsuits. Today's music business is so complicated, we need a return to simpler forms of doing business.

## Independence And Co-operation

While trust is desirable, it is also advisable to maintain a certain amount of independence from your manager. You should have a different attorney and a different accountant from the ones he uses. In fact, you shouldn't really enter into a deal with someone using the same attorney, because it destroys the protection that an attorney affords you. If you find yourself about to do business with another client of your attorney's, it may be advisable to hire another attorney to represent you in that agreement. The same is basically true for accountants. An accountant is the man you trust to handle your money. You are, in a sense, trusting him to favor you over your manager, your record company, and everyone else you deal with. His other clients expect him to do the same for them, so your doing business with them can compromise his position. These things are easily worked out, but it is good to be aware of them.

Beyond having a separate attorney and accountant, there isn't too much you can do to be independent of your manager without jeopardizing the highly personalized nature of the relationship. In order to be competitive with major acts, you're going to have to spend so much time working on your music that you can't afford to be checking up on your manager. You have to trust someone to take care of all your business, and if you have doubts about him, get someone else. Think of the word *manage*. To manage means to control. You are letting someone else *control* your career. You have to have a good relationship with your manager, because you are turning your entire career (including the dreams) over to him. You'd better have confidence in him.

A manager can make or break your career, but he is only as strong as the act he is representing. If you go on stage and do your job at night, and he gets on the phone and does his job during the day, it's magic. In the beginning it's important to work on building your rapport with him. Get to know him. You don't have to be best friends with him, but you need to know how he thinks. You need to communicate with him about what you expect (See Chapter 11) and you need to study him to see if he fulfills those expectations. Does he follow up on the things he says? Money talks, bullshit walks. Of course, real rapport will only come after you work with your manager for a while on a daily basis.

It is also important to remember to let your manager do his job. Establish a regular schedule of communication, and then trust him to take care of business. Don't be calling him every day to hound him. He's a pro and he won't appreciate your prodding. Of course, you can't just let him waltz away your life, either. You have to learn the difference between communication and hounding, and between making suggestions and trying to tell someone how to do their job. This will take time and effort. Any relationship has growing pains and requires some work and discernment. Working with a manager is no different.

## Being A Manager

It takes a special kind of person to be a manager. You have to be high-powered and sensitive at the same time. Besides the wheeling and dealing, it is also a baby-sitting gig, and you'd better realize that you're going to get calls at four in the morning. It's real nice to wake up to a screaming voice telling you that the band was late to the gig and the club owner is refusing to pay, or that they overturned the truck in Keokuk and they want you to wire them the money to fix it. You have to get used to being yelled at when you're a manager. The reason so many managers yell a lot is that they've been on the receiving end for so long, they start responding in kind. It's not a lot of fun to have to listen to some promoter scream at you because you booked a band too close to his gig, or to be sued because one of your acts didn't show up. Realize that being a manager is hard work and requires you to put up with a lot of hassle.

Most big time managers start out as small time managers with small time artists whom they travel on the road with, learning the ropes and making contacts. They work the box office, get to know the agents and promoters, the club owners, the disc jockeys, and then they get lucky with one act. All it takes is one big act to make you a big-time manager. Of course, getting lucky with an act when you're a small time manager is pretty rare. Often, managers start out as agents or promoters and score in those areas. Other times they may work their way up in a record company and then leave to manage an act. It doesn't matter how you do it, as long as you learn the knowledge and develop the clout. Sometimes a small-time manager will have a great act which he can turn over to a big name manager, and join the big name's company as an assistant. The small manager merges with Irv Azoff, Jeff Wald, Shep Gordon, or someone like that, and they give him an office in their company. More importantly, they give him the right to use their name. It is amazing how much the same guy can get done with the clout of a big name manager behind him. He might even stay with the act he brought in and just split the percentage with the name manager's company, or even take a lesser percentage. This is a very good way for a talented young manager to work his way into the big time. If you are good, but you haven't yet had the big breakthrough, aligning yourself with a winner may be the way to go, as long as you leave yourself room to operate and keep your self-respect.

If you want to be a manager, the best way to begin is to jump in and start doing it. There is no formalized training, but there are a lot of areas that can give you the right experience. If you can get a job working for an agency or a management firm, that is probably the best way to begin, but you can also get valuable experience promoting small shows in your home town or working at a nightclub. Any work that you can do in the field of popular music will help you, because a manager has to know a little about everything. Even jobs in advertising or sales can give you needed experience that can later be applied to developing artists. It will take some time, but don't rush it. Just like an artist, you need to take it a step at a time.

A manager must know people. His real strength is in his contacts. Contrary to what most people believe, the best way to develop contacts is not by meeting people at the top. It's by meeting people who are *on their way* to the top. The powerful managers of today used to be struggling just the way you are now. The time to befriend them would have been when they needed you. A person remembers those who can help him up the ladder, so realize that those on your level today may be the powerhouses of the industry tomorrow. When you're talking to a local deejay in Kankakee, Illinois, understand that five years from now he might be an influencial program director in Chicago. When you meet the twenty year old whiz kid with three record stores in Philadelphia, don't be surprised if he has fifty of them before he's thirty. The engineer at your local four track may one day be the hottest producer in Hollywood. If you treat the people you meet with respect (even the "unimportant" ones), you will have more contacts than you know what to do with in a few years. You always hear about somebody stepping all over everyone on his way to the top, but those people don't last as long as the ones who make friends along the way. Clout is having contacts, and contacts are friends with power. It's not easy to make friends with people who have power unless you meet them before they have it. Sure, you want to "get in" with the big boys, but don't ignore the others. Some of them will undoubtedly get where they want to go, and when they do, you want to be on their good side.

Becoming a manager is like most things in the music business. It takes a lot of hard work, experience, and talent. There is no formal education for any position in this business (unless you count engineering school and the six years that an attorney spends learning how to intimidate people). One of the things that you must learn from experience is how to be discerning about talent and dedication. First you must discern your own, and then you must learn to gauge these elements in the acts you work with. The faster you learn how to do this, the less time you will waste. New managers spend a lot of time working with acts they like, who turn out not to be as good as they thought. Or else they spend six months of hard work getting an artist to the point where they are ready for the big time, only to have him quit the business. I can't teach you how to recognize or protect yourself from these kinds of mistakes, but be aware of them. *Be discerning!* Learn to be a hard judge of talent. It is better to underestimate than overestimate an artist's abilities. Learn to take their ambition with a grain of salt as well. An artist can't tell you how dedicated he is, because that is only something which can be shown. When the going gets tough, how quick do they begin to give up?

You have to be aggressive as a manager, but you don't have to be a monster. Communication solves more problems than arguing. Being a manager is a tough enough gig without making

any unnecessary enemies. Your loyalty is to your artist, and
you must fight, if necessary, to protect him, but beyond that,
try not to get carried away with being a tough guy.

### Attorneys: When You Need One and When You Don't

You need an attorney about the same time you need a manager. In other words, when your act is *ready*. When you have to
negotiate and interpret contracts in the upper levels of the
music business, it is essential that you have a good attorney.
You can handle the contract for the Bradley-Bourbonnais High
School "Sock-Hop" yourself, but when it comes to signing with
a label, get some professional help. Getting the right attorney
can be one of the best moves you will ever make because,
besides providing you with legal representation, he can also
connect you with the right people to help your career. A good
music business attorney has contacts coming out of his ears.
He may represent a few major artists, managers, producers,
and even record labels. If he likes your work, he can plug you
in to the big time easier than you can say "consultation fee."

Of course, there are some shyster attorneys, so if the advice
you're getting doesn't seem right, check it out with someone
else. If a doctor told you he was going to have to amputate
your tongue, you'd sure as hell get a second opinion before you
let him whack it off, wouldn't you? Think of your career in
the same way.

### Finding The Right One

A good music business attorney is as hard to get as a good
manager. First of all, you want someone who is educated in
music law. Most lawyers don't know beans about music business law, so make that your first qualification. Secondly, you
want someone who is active in the music business. Anyone
who knows much about the music business will usually get in
on the action after a while because of the tremendous amount
of money to be made. The first time an attorney hears a great
song for a big name artist he is representing, being played by

an unknown song writer, you can bet he is already filling out forms to start a publishing company. It's too easy not to. So you want an attorney who knows how the game is played, because he has gone around a few times himself. It would really help you to find an attorney who is already handling other major artists. In addition to his opening up a few doors, it also means that he obviously knows what he is doing.

Finding the right attorney is like finding the right anything. You have to shop for it. Check out a few attorneys and pick the one you like best. If you have a record deal on the horizon, most of these guys should at least sit down and talk to you. If you are totally unknown, it can be difficult getting an appointment to see the big boys. If you're rich, just make consultation appointments and pay fees all day until you find the man you want. Of course, if you're rich, you might just ask your father's attorney whom he recommends. The only way to get to an important attorney (or manager, or agent), is by meeting him somewhere, or by meeting someone who can refer you to him. The second way is much more likely. If Johnny Swartzbottom is a hot enough act to have a top manager and attorney, and Johnny likes your music, ask him to open the door for you. Make the rounds and contact all the heavies, but don't be surprised if that doesn't get you anywhere. You've got to learn to knock on doors in this business without getting upset when nobody answers.

Once you are talking with a top attorney, there are certain things you can look for in him. The main thing is how he makes you feel. Does he scare you? If you feel intimidated because the guy is always pointing to his diplomas or his gold records, and treating you like you were an amoeba, you'd better leave before he destroys your self-confidence. On the other hand, maybe you want an attorney who is intimidating and treats everybody like they were idiots. Some folks like to have people like that on their side, even if they do feel uncomfortable around them. In most cases, however, you will want an attorney who makes you feel good. You need to feel comfortable with anyone who is involved with your career. You need to feel that they really care about you and your talent.

By the way, if you are an aspiring manager or other music businessman, you also need an attorney. Roughly the same qualifications hold true except that, in many ways, an attorney is to you what a personal manager might be to an artist. So, if you're a businessman, it is even more important that your attorney is willing to introduce you to people who can benefit your career.

## Dealing With Attorneys

Needless to say, most attorneys are very proper about business practices. You have to be more "businesslike" in dealing with them than you do with some other professionals. That doesn't mean that attorneys don't have a sense of humor. They do have a sense of humor (they just don't laugh during business hours). Most attorneys will want to work by fees, and these can be pretty expensive. After you've worked with an attorney long enough for him to recognize your potential, he might agree to take a flat 5% of your career for doing all your legal work. This is much better for you because it means the attorney *will* use his connections to help your career. Of course, there are no prescribed rules here either, and your method of paying the attorney can be anything that you both agree to.

## Agents & Promoters: Finding & Being One

*"We weren't even expecting 100,000 people, and more than that were waiting in the field the first day. When I told my engineer to build a bridge from the crowd to the artists, he asked me how much Jimmy Hendrix weighed. He figured the maximum load would be Jimmy Hendrix being chased by a bridge full of groupies. He was right. There were problems at Woodstock, but it could have been a lot worse."*

**—John Morris** (one of the promoters of Woodstock)*

* © Rock-Pop, 5/27/79

A good agent is one who will *work* for you, but the major agents can't do anything for you unless you have a record contract. They can, however, help you get a contract and in that sense they should be regarded as managers. All that nonsense about opening for a major act doesn't happen unless the record company or manager sticks you on the bill.

The other way you can get major concert exposure is through a promoter. Since you won't be drawing anyone to the concert in comparison with the main attraction, the promoter will be doing you a favor to let you open for the name act. He may not even pay you, and will probably only do it if he is stuck for an opener at the last minute. You can also get exposure by being managed by a promoter, and in that case regard him in that way (as you may have guessed, anyone with power can make a good attempt at managing. It takes more than power to succeed, but that sure is a great place to start). Once you have a deal and are ready to tour the country, have your manager or agent contact the top promoters in the country and try to line up a date for you.

If you want to be an agent, you will have to learn the same kinds of things that a prospective manager must learn. As an agent, you will work with artists and their managers in selling acts to club owners and promoters. Agents often start out as little league managers working the bar set. When they get one act working a lot, they start developing and booking another. Pretty soon they have their own agency. It takes this kind of experience and plenty of contacts to crack the big time agencies, but once you know the ropes, you can work your way into such a job if you really want it.

If you want to be a promoter, you have to learn what it takes to have a successful concert. You may have to do it on a small scale, but the principles are the same. You have to learn how and when to advertise, what acts to hire, how to market tickets, set up security, provide sound and lighting, and make it all work together for the enjoyment of the crowd. Promoting a successful show at your local recreation hall takes the same kind of knowledge as doing one at the L.A. Forum. If you really want to be a promoter, you'll keep on working your way up and learning all along the way. It takes a lot of guts to be a promoter because it's your money that is on the line. But, promoting concerts is also one of the few ways left to get outrageously rich in a relatively short amount of time. Just remember to take your time and *pay attention to detail.* It would also do you good to work with a big time promoter in any capacity as long as you can watch what they are doing (it's pretty hard to watch what goes on at the front office when you're selling peanuts in the stands).

A lot of managers have been agents and promoters. Jerry Weintraub and Irving Azoff are two who began by doing both, on a smaller scale. There is no formula for *anything* in the music business other than experience and contacts, so if you want to be a manager, agent, or promoter, get out there and *do* it.

# Chapter 10
# Record Labels, Radio, Charts, & Critics

*"When we were ready to record the "Crime of the Century" album, we had to reignite the interest of the record company. After two albums that didn't do very well, they were beginning to have doubts about the band. Fortunately, they liked the early stuff they heard from "Crime" and that renewed their commitment enough to support the record. It turned out to be our breaking point."*

—**John Heliwell,**
**Supertramp**\*

## How A Record Label Is Structured

Like most large businesses, a record label is broken down into departments which function together under an organized chain of command. At the top is the president of the label, or the chairman of the board, depending upon the size of the company. Underneath him is a vice-president (or president if the top man is chairman of the board), who functions as a general manager. He is usually the man who makes the wheels turn

\* © *Rock-Pop, 5/28/78*

and keeps the company going on a day to day basis. He does this by communicating with the various department heads. These are also usually vice-presidents and they are responsible for different segments of the company. The official names of these departments can vary and they can be combined in a variety of ways, but a general breakdown would be as follows:

Artists & Repertoire (A & R), Artist Relations, Advertising, Art Department, Business Affairs, Legal, Promotion, Publicity, Publishing, and Sales.

The Sales Department may be lumped with Promotion under the title of Marketing, and Publicity may be grouped with the Art Department and Advertising under the heading of Creative Services. In addition, the Marketing Division may be broken down into pop, country, and R & B departments (some labels even have jazz and classical departments).

Artists & Repertoire is the creative end of the company where new artist acquisitions are made (if a genie pops out of your beer bottle one afternoon, one of the wishes you want is power over the A & R Department of your favorite label). The A & R Department also determines the budgets for album projects. The division is composed of staff producers and their assistants. There are variations in all companies and the specific job titles vary notoriously in the music business. Warner Records, for example, has a concept which they call *Professional Manager.* He is under the A & R Department and manages a certain block of acts for the label. He helps them acquire material, assists in the studio, helps with the artwork, and performs various other functions. He is the act's manager at the label, and he helps them not get lost in the shuffle of departments, by overseeing everything at the label related to that act. Other labels have something similar which they call artist relations, and people from this department also travel on the road with the artist.

The Art and Advertising Departments need no explanation. Business Affairs may include the Legal Department, and it is in charge of all the business operations of the label, including accounting.

The Promotion Department primarily deals with promoting product to radio stations and record stores. Publicity is concerned with promoting product to magazines, newspapers, and the various critics. They also set up interviews, and that means that they occasionally deal with radio stations and record stores.

Many labels have publishing firms and these may or may not operate out of the same offices as the label. The Sales Department is just that, and it also includes distribution.

The different departments at a record label all cross each other's path in various ways. In the overall power scheme, the heads of the departments are pretty much equal in the sense that any of them can be promoted over the others. It all depends upon who has the ear of the president. There are a lot of crazy situations at labels where the guy who is head of the Art Department suddenly becomes head of A & R, or a publicist becomes Director of Talent Acquisition. A lot of this is brown-nosing, but an equal amount is good, solid work.

## Getting The Job

There are a lot of ways to get a job at a record label, and almost all of them are through a personal contact. The required background may be different, but the method of getting the job is pretty similar. Like any job, you have to apply, but it really helps if you know somebody at the label who has enough clout to get you in the door. In fact there aren't too many ways of getting around the old friends and relatives who are in line ahead of you, unless you're one yourself. Experience really helps of course, but you have to start somewhere, and most doors are shut tight. Unfortunately, resumés that aren't accompanied by a personal recommendation are filed under "T" for trash.

Education is another factor. What having a degree in journalism has to do with being a publicist is a question I can't answer, but it helps in getting the job (then again, I don't know what having a degree in journalism has to do with being a journalist, either). At any rate, having a degree helps. Of course, if you knew the vice-president's sister, that would be more important.

To get a job at a record company, you must be able to get along well with people (you also must be able to get along well with people to *stand* working at a record company). There is a lot of bullshit to put up with, and one of the things that makes up for it is enjoying small talk and semi-friendships. It is a misconception that working at a label is one big party. There is a lot of hard work to be done, and sometimes even the parties are serious business. Most of the people at a label are somewhat social creatures. There may be a few lone rangers in the Art or A&R Departments, but they are few and far between. So, plan on smiling a lot and being cordial to *everybody* if you want to be part of a record company.

In order to give you further background information on working for a label, I will discuss a few of the jobs in depth. Since the actual acquiring of the job is very similar, no matter what department you are in, I will describe the day to day activities of some of the various jobs so that you can determine your qualifications. (Wow! This book is finally starting to sound like some sort of textbook. I wonder if it's too late to get serious?)

## Publicists

Besides being a secretary and packing records in the warehouse, one job that may be availalbe to you is that of publicist. Publicists work for the head of the Publicity Department and their day is spent making phone calls to hype records to reviewers, set up interviews with artists, and arrange press junkets and parties. They also spend a good deal of time writing bios and press releases and answering the somewhat strange requests of pop music writers. Sometimes a publicist will travel on the road with an artist to arrange and oversee interviews. Most publicists are talented writers and they usually come from the field of rock journalism. They may start out at a newspaper or magazine, reviewing records and, after making some good contacts at the label, move in when there is an opening. Publicists make between fifteen and eighteen grand a year, and they earn it. Often their evenings are spent at concerts or clubs "helping" reviewers enjoy the show and introducing them to artists. This sounds exciting, but it can get to be a real drag real fast.

## Promotion Department

Getting the record played on the radio is what makes it all happen. If you have the innate ability to get along with radio people well enough to get them to play records, you can earn a fortune as a record label promotion man. Promotion men are paid by their ability to get results. They're not on a commission, but the more airplay they get, the more salary they can command. In many ways, a promotion man is an independent businessman, in that he often doesn't have to work out of an office. Promotion men are scattered all over the country in different "territories." They make their calls on radio stations and record stores and report in to the label each day with the results.

It is a myth that promotion men say things like, "Listen baby, I've got some wax here that will melt your socks." Actually they say things like, "I wouldn't kid you about this one, it's the tightest groove I've ever heard." There is a difference, but you would have to be in the business for the last ten years to recognize it. Promo men like to sell, and their biggest problem is not always being able to turn off the hype when they want to (you've probably all heard about the promo man who told his girlfriend that he loved her "with a bullet").

Record companies rarely hire an untried promotion man because the job is far too important to risk on an amateur. Most promotion men start out working for independent distributors who may handle several labels in a given city. From there they might go to working for a major label in the distribution wing focusing on the same city where they have already established contacts. The whole secret to being a promotion man is developing rapport with disc jockeys. A lot of promotion men, in fact, are ex-disc jockeys themselves. Still others are ex-musicians, agents, managers, and promoters (I realize that there is no such thing as an ex-musician. I just threw that in there to see if you were paying attention). It also helps to have sales experience.

Sometimes a fair door-to-door vacuum salesman will make a great promotion man because he knows how to push for the sale and it is easier dealing with a radio programmer than an irate housewife (When a programmer slams the door in your face, his secretary apologizes for him).

There are four main levels of both promotion and sales. The *international* level is usually handled through liaisons with foreign companies. (Incidentally, about 60% of the world record market is *outside* of the U.S., so stop laughing because it only takes something like twenty thousand records to get a gold album in Norway. It adds up.) The *national* level is overseen by the National Promotion Director. He's the guy who yells at all the *regional* directors when the records aren't charting. The regional people are then expected to scream at the *local* promotion and sales people. Sales people often start out at a record store and then get an office job with a label at their warehouse and so on.

In addition to these areas, record companies often have different promotion men for different kinds of music. It's better to have a country music fan talk with the country music stations, a jazz fan for the jazz stations, and a Dick Contino fan for the accordian stations. Smaller companies (of which there may be none left by this writing) often only have one man in each major market, and he concentrates on pop product unless there is some "crossover" action in another market.

## A & R

If you want to work in the A&R Department, you are probably a musical person. You like to listen to music and you are infatuated with what makes a hit record a hit. You should also have an eye for spotting talent in slightly unpolished form (I say "slightly" because there are so many acts out there who are working hard on polishing themselves that A & R people merely have to look for the cream of the crop). It *is* important to recognize a hit song in its less developed form because many "gems" may come in on cheap cassettes with poor vocals. Most A&R men miss these, but the best turn them into big bucks.

Getting a job in A&R is not easy. Having friends at the label is even more important for jobs that have less formalized experience. There are not many jobs that you can have which give you good A&R experience. Being a disco deejay, a radio programmer, or a promoter could help you, but each one only gives you half of the experience you need. An A&R man needs to recognize both a good record and a good live act. He wants his groups to have both of these elements and part of his job is to help them develop both areas.

Getting a job as an A&R man means that someone at the label thinks you can spot talent. Since this is not an exact science they are, more or less, giving you a shot to see how you will do. This is true in every job, but it is more true in A & R. Of course, since results are difficult to gauge, it will be pretty hard for the label to determine if you really are doing your job. Consequently, your job becomes more one of "seeing" acts than "recognizing" talent. It is more a job of "listening" to tapes than "hearing" hits.

Some of the most talented people in this business are A&R men. In many cases, they are the ones who keep the record companies in business. Each label usually has one guy with "ears" and it is his judgment which keeps them alive. As an artist, you want to get your tape in the hands of these men, but to do that, unfortunately, often means you have to get past a few flunkies who also call themselves A&R men. A lot of staff A&R guys are basic flunkies who are there as buffers to keep away all the undesirables. Their job is to give you a courteous listen and send you on your way before you waste the time of somebody important. This is a needed function in any business as "glamorous" as ours. Unfortunately, the people in these positions also keep away some of the major talents of our age. Who are they? How should I know, I never got to hear them.

The record companies operate on the theory that, since they cannot adequately screen everybody who walks in the door, they are bound to lose a few potential stars. On the other hand, they figure that if the act is really hot, they will hear about it from another source. This is the all-important *"well-respected source"* rule which states that a record company will listen much more closely and objectively to any tape that is referred to them by a well-respected source. Well-respected sources can be managers, attorneys, agents, promoters, other artists, producers, deejays, promotion men, department heads, fish market managers, or apple turn-over jugglers. In short, they can be anyone that the label's execs and the A&R man with the "ears" respects. Sometimes they can even be the wife or kid brother of someone the label respects, depending on how much they respect them (the respectee that is, or is it the respector?). Ninety-nine and nine-tenths percent of the acts which come in off the street are rejected, and the acts which are signed are the ones referred from another source. Please don't ask what the percentage of rejection is for tapes that come in the mail. It's something like a thousand percent (ten tapes are sent back for every one that comes in). There are exceptions, but don't plan on being one of them.

If you want to be an A&R man (even a flunkie A&R man), you will have to face the same difficulties that an artist faces. The reason the music business is so tough to break into, is that it is a continuous circle among proven individuals. To get a chance to play, you have to have played before, which makes starting out very difficult. To get into the game, therefore, you have to get a break. If the break is big enough, you become a proven individual and from then on you can play the game with a full deck of cards (unless you've gone crazy from the experience). This is also pretty much the way the well-respected source rule works. To get a well-respected source, you have to be referred by another well-respected source and so on, in typical music business circle fashion (after all, they taught the army how to play Catch-22).

Let's take two "equal" acts to illustrate the rule in action. Eddie Ears, the hot A&R man at Bomb Records, gets a call from his attorney telling him about a great local band called "The Bile." Eddie makes a mental note, but he is too busy to do anything more. Two weeks later, Chuck Cashflow, the president of the label is contacted by his old friend about the same band. Chuck sends a memo to Eddie telling him to check out "The Bile" at the Starwood that week. Eddie is still too busy (hot A&R men are *always* too busy), so he forwards the memo to Sammy

Slack, his A&R flunkie. Sammy is flabbergasted. He rushes down to the Starwood that week and is totally blown away by the band before he hears their first tune. The next day, he raves them up to Eddie and contract negotiations are begun. That same afternoon, Jimmy Wax walks in from Des Moines with his tape. It is his third visit, so Sammy agrees to see him. He hates the tape and manages to not hear a note of it. Jimmy Wax leaves dejected, intending to go back to Des Moines and get a job at Burger King, and "The Bile" are the new rage of L.A. Both acts are equal in talent and commercial potential, but "The Bile" succeeded because of the well-respected source rule.

If you are an artist, you have to get yourself a well-respected source. If you want to be an A&R man, you have to use it to your advantage without letting it destroy your objectivity. Hopefully, you want to do more than just keep your job. Hopefully, you want to discover and develop real talent. A&R flunkies often start out as men with vision who get scared and wind up just holding a job. When that happens, they draw a salary for being detrimental to the quality and integrity of the music business. What is saddest about the above story is that both Sammy Slack and Jimmy Wax think that Sammy is at the label to discover new talent. He is no longer there for that at all. He is there to fill a space at a desk.

## Executive Material

The people who wind up as top executives at a label are the people who learn to play the game the best. They have learned a little about everything that goes on at the label and they have managed to get close to the important people without stepping on too many toes. If you want to be an executive, you first have to get a job at the label and figure out its power structure (which is not as easy as it sounds). You have to get close to the big acts and the top executives. You need to show that you function well in a power play situation and that you are willing to sacrifice almost everything for the good of the label. It also helps to do something "unforgettable" like bring in a saviour act which keeps the label from folding, or something equally heavy. If you want to be a label president, you have to do all these things consistently well for a few years.

If you become President of the label, realize that the label will be your life. It will be very difficult to sustain any other interests, and that includes a wife and children. It is a gruelling job with incredible pressure which leaves very little time to enjoy any financial or personal satisfaction derived from it.

It's much more fun to *pretend* to be the president of the label. Just get yourself a Gucci bag, some dark glasses, a tennis visor, and learn to say very little while nodding your head a lot. Then show up at the labels and nod hello to everyone. Just walk around all day on the various floors and you'll be surprised at how many of the new secretaries play up to you. If you really want to go all the way, get a tee-shirt with the letters BMAL printed on the front (Big Man At Label).

While trying to get a job at a label can be very frustrating, it can also lead to a rewarding and satisfying career. Actually, when you consider the various straight jobs that are available, working for a record label has to be one of the best. While it is not as loose as most people think, it is still less restrictive than most other jobs. The pay is above average and the opportunity for growth is definitely there. More than any of the other things I've mentioned except the buddy system, persistence is what will land you a job at a label. There are a lot of labels out there and if you keep making yourself and your desire to work for one known, eventually you'll get in. Don't be a pest, but don't give up either.

## Radio

Landing a record deal is getting in the game, securing good management is getting the ball, but you have to do well on the radio to score a touchdown. Almost nobody buys a record he hasn't heard at least part of, and absolutely no one risks seven or eight bucks on an act they don't know from Adam. The key to sales, of course, is exposure, and the key to exposure is radio. A few groups have been able to maintain consistent record sales without a lot of airplay, but only after they were able to secure a loyal following through live performances. And initially what got the people to those live performances was radio.

The man you want to influence at a radio station is the Music Director. He decides, as his title suggests, what music gets played on the station. At smaller stations the Music Director may also be the Program Director. The Program Director is responsible for everything that goes on the air, including newscasts, commercials, programs, and music. At the smaller stations, he is the man who has to like your record for it to get on the air. At the larger stations, he works in conjunction with the Music Director, so it is good to have both men behind your record. Some PD's (hip radio talk for Program Directors) allow their Music Directors more leeway than others (MD by the way is not-so-hip slang for doctor).

Radio programmers are influenced by a variety of things, which include trade magazines, tip sheets, other radio stations, and promotion men. The trade magazines are described under the next section ("Charts"). Tip sheets are reports of radio airplay collected from several stations and grouped in various categories. Radio programmers subscribe to tipsheets because they help them keep up with other stations. The bigger stations are affected by what is happening in the secondary market stations, particularly the ones that are near their area. Tip sheets also chart records according to airplay and contain recommendations and reviews.

The promotion department of a record company works on a major radio station in a variety of ways. The national director may call the station and tell them to watch for a particular new release. The local man would bring in the new releases and single out a few of them to the programmer as being especially worthy of his attention. A few days later, the regional director might call to find out how the programmer feels about the record. Working together, the various elements of the promotion department can exert considerable persuasion on radio stations. It might begin with the National Director calling an old friend of his who runs a station in Oxnard, Ca. and asking him to play a new release "as a favor." A week later he might call another friend in Columbus and persuade him to play the record because of the action it is getting in Oxnard. Now he has a couple of good markets "on" the record, plus all the results the regional and local people have been pulling in. Before you know it, he successfully pitches a major station in Chicago and the record hits the charts at Number 60 with a bullet in Billboard.

A lot of promoting records is combining hype and results into a successful word-of-mouth pitch. When you see an ad in Billboard or Cashbox, for example, don't think its purpose is to convince radio programmers to play the record, as much as it is to impress them with the idea that the label is behind the record. Programmers pay more attention when they know the label is shelling out big bucks. When you combine this hype with the press the act is generating by being on the road, and the efforts of the promotion men, things start to happen. When the promo man in Chicago gets a new batch of releases, he will take them to the big gun stations first, on the long shot that they might go for one of them without established action. Even if they don't, he has still implanted the fact that Sammy Podunk & The Pizzas have a hot new record out. The promo man's next stop is the lesser markets in his area (Joliet, Peoria, Indianapolis, South Bend, Springfield, Rock Island, Rockford, and Johannesburg, South Africa—some of these guys got pretty big territories). He'll also be watching the tip sheets and getting additional input from his label on where the record is being played. He uses this information, the results of the act's tour, and anything else he can, to resell the major station. If he has been able to successfully "surround" it with airplay at the other stations in the area, getting the major to go should be easy. With this kind of thing happening all over the country, the promotion department is able to get a snowball effect going which can take them right to the top of the charts.

By the way, *never* take your own record to a radio station. Representing yourself at a station tells the programmer that the record label isn't behind you, and if they don't have confidence in you, why should he? He listens to the best pitches in the business all week long, and then you come in there with your record and a dumb smile on your face. You expect him to be impressed? He doesn't care about meeting you. He is only interested in the sound of his station and he is looking for records that fit in with that sound because that affects his ratings. And the ratings affect the amount of advertising dollars that come in, and that affects his job. No matter how small your label is, you should be able to get somebody to take the record in to stations for you. I've already told you how worthless releasing your own record is, and promoting it yourself is even worse.

Radio programmers are concerned that the record label will put out the effort to make sure albums are in the stores, and advertise them when they get there (maybe even on his station). A programmer might be courteous enough to listen to your record, but after you leave, he will use it to set drinks on. Your presence at his station is telling him that nobody else is willing to promote your record. There are a lot of secondary, tershendary, and fourthendary markets with little radio stations that may be more prone to play unknown records by unknown artists on unknown labels. There aren't too many of them though, and your best bets are the ones near your home town. Even promoting these stations is bad business because you can never represent yourself as well as someone else can. If you don't rave up the record, the guy will figure it isn't any good, and if you tell him how great it is, he'll think you're a conceited snob.

## Charts

*"Number six is actually worse than number seven, because number six is only one away from the Top Five. I was at number two for three weeks and that was worse than being number three, because it was so close to number one. Number One means a lot of things like the Johnny Carson Show and all kinds of other exposure."*
**—Yvonne Elliman***

Charts are the measuring stick that record labels and radio stations use to determine the success of a record. The ultimate criterion, of course, is sales, but the music industry requires a more immediate form of measurement. The charts are designed

* © *Rock-Pop 8/7/78*

to report and predict sales *while* they are happening. There are many different charts and they all have a slightly different formula for compilation. Some of them place more emphasis on radio airplay and requests, while others focus more on sales.

The most widely read charts are in the three most popular trade magazines (Billboard, Cashbox, and Record World). All three monitor radio stations and record stores through reports. Their methods are highly secretive, as many labels would give an awful lot to "sabotage" them to their advantage. The charts protect their accuracy by changing their sources on a regular basis. Perhaps they receive reports from fifty stores in a particular market, for example, but each week they only add twenty-five of them into the results. By changing which twenty-five stores are used each week, they can minimize the effect of "dumping." Dumping is giving away records to stores in return for them reporting sales.

Each major label has a specialist who does nothing but hype the trade magazines and tipsheets. His job is to party with them and feed them information in an effort to get the record a "bullet," or at least on the charts. This is one indication of how important the charts are to the success of a record. Getting "action" in the trades and tipsheets means that more stations will play the record. More stations playing the record means it will move up the charts and get still more stations to play it. Pretty soon the sales start rolling in and the snowball really gets going. Some people criticize the charts for relying so much on airplay rather than just actual sales, but this is an effort to "keep ahead of the public," which is very important to radio stations. There is no denying that getting records on the charts is what all the vast and intricate machinery of a record label is designed to do. Getting to Number One is the second wish you ask the genie for.

## Critics

Critics are not as important as most people think, and nowhere near as important as most critics believe. Unfortunately, being pompous and self-inflated is a built-in weakness for a critic. He has to think his opinion is important in order to do his job.

The publicity department of a record label zeros in on the important critics with every new release. The important critics are those with the numbers and prestige. The big circulation newspapers and magazines are the most influential because they reach the most people. Some magazines have established a reputation that exceeds their circulation power. A favorable review in Rolling Stone, for example, is more important than one in a newspaper that reaches twice the number of people, because Rolling Stone has established a reputation for expertise in pop music which record labels can play to the hilt in advertisements.

Critics affect an artist's image more than they affect his actual sales. The public formulates their opinions about an artist by reading reviews and interviews, but they buy their records based on what they hear on the radio. Very few people will rush out and buy an album because someone they don't know in a newspaper raves it up. Of course, they might ask their favorite store to pop it on the turntable for a quick listen. In general, critics have nowhere near the power that radio stations enjoy.

Naturally, critics have more power over an unknown act, but most critics do not pan unknowns. If the critic doesn't like a new band, he may just refuse to write about it. The exceptions are those acts which receive so much hype from the label that the public becomes interested. A critic can really be a valuable friend to a new act because he can give them the recognition that they so badly need (critics have a tendency to "adopt" certain new bands like they were pets. The critic makes it his personal project to get the group off the ground, and often it will work). One thing I don't like about some critics is that they often take pot-shots at artists who are successful, simply because they are doing well. It seems that all the critics have secret meetings and decide "whats-his-name has gotten good reviews from all of us for his last three albums, so we've got to get him with this one."

Critics are some of the most knowledgeable people in the music business. Many of them are experts at guessing how the public will respond to a new record. Others are equally talented at analyzing and dissecting the various elements that go into a "good" record. Some critics are true patrons of the arts and they regularly call an artist to task for not fulfilling his artistic responsibilities. There is no such thing as an expert in a business that is based on matters of taste, but critics are about as close as you can come. NOTE: Don't freak out if a critic hates your record. Bad reviews sometimes make an album sell bigger because everyone wants to know what all the fuss is about.

# Chapter 11
# More About The Business End

*"I can see that the Beatles meant so much to people. The Beatles were good, like a good cake, and when it was broken down into its separate pieces they were only average. Getting back together is not beyond the bounds of possibility, but we've gone such separate ways, it would be like expecting us to go back to school or something. Maybe it will happen, but it won't be because of people bringing pressure on us. It's not our responsibility to live up to demands like that. In the beginning, being a Beatle was great, but after a while it became ridiculous. There was no privacy at all. We became owned by the world."*

**—George Harrison***

### Dealmakers: The Creative Businessmen

In the previous chapters I have talked a little about managers, attorneys, agents, promoters, record company executives, and record producers. All of these people are businessmen, and as you may have guessed by my descriptions of them, they often

* © *Rock-Pop, 12/26/76*

overlap in their various functions. One quality you should be sure is a part of everyone you work closely with, is the ability to be a creative businessman. The people you do business with should be as creative in their field as you are in yours. It is a huge misconception that all the creativity in the music business belongs to the artists.

If you look at the history of the Beatles, you will see that the creative genius of Brian Epstein played as important a role in their success as that of Paul McCartney or John Lennon. The music industry is filled with guys who are absolute marvels in the way they do business. They have imagination and the ability to apply that imagination in an original way, to succeed at the art of business. You won't get very far if you take the attitude that conducting business is for boring dolts who can only understand art from the point of view of an observer rather than a participant. Some of these guys are *artists* in what they do. To succeed, it is important to be able to recognize and appreciate these qualities in your associates. I would like to explore the differences between a creative businessman and your typical fish-faced pencil pusher (or worse yet, a super aggressive "used car" type).

A creative businessman creates his own market. He is an entrepreneur in the true sense, in that he is in control of as many variables as possible. In music, a creative businessman doesn't take the attitude that there is nothing he can do because "the market is tight" or "the labels put a freeze on new signings." That's a pencil-pusher attitude. He also doesn't lie his way in to see somebody and then try to yell his way into a deal. That's a used car approach. A creative businessman finds a creative way to approach the label and interest them, despite the current market conditions. Sometimes of course there really is very little that a person can do, but most of the time, all you hear about "money being tight" means you haven't come up with the right angle. People are always ready to make money, and record companies are always willing to spend a little if you can successfully convince them that they can make a lot.

People who are not creative businessmen run up against a lot of "insurmountable" walls in this business, because they are easily discouraged. In fact, if you are easily discouraged, you'd better forget the music business, because it is one of the most discouraging professions in the world. Some of the most successful people in the music industry have substituted aggression for determination, and I must admit it works pretty well. But if you have to be angry all the time in order to succeed, who wants to?

Creative businessmen are geniuses at putting the right combinations together. They match up acts with labels, writers with artists, managers with attorneys, and rich kids with no talent with poor kids who have oodles of it. Pairing you up with the right person or company can make a huge difference in your career.

A creative businessman comes in many forms. He can be your manager, the guy in artist relations at the label, a club owner, the owner of a music store, or just about anything else. He has a virtual fountain of ideas, and loves what he is doing. He also usually does it well enough to make a nice living at it.

There is also such a thing as being more creative than you have the business sense to handle. A creative businessman has to have a sense of balance or else he'll always be the "kid with great ideas who has never been able to make any of them work." If that's you at this moment, then you had better learn to focus your energy, because that is probably the problem. Some guys are so creative that they never follow an idea all the way through before a "better" one takes its place. You have to have a certain discipline to do business. Creative people who become attorneys usually do very well in the music business, because they are trained in discipline enough to let their creative capacity go nuts and still "keep on the beam." I guess if I had to choose between an unimaginative plod and a half-skitzo creative genius to promote my career, I'd take the skitzo, but the idea is to have the best of both. Both the attention to detail *and* the imagination. The spark to come up with a great plan *and* the strength to see it through.

To help you apply creative business, let me give you a few examples. A "small-time" one is the local manager who wanted his act to have the distinction of being the number one band in their medium sized home town. He knew they were great on stage, but how was he going to get the rest of the town to know? He could have booked them twenty small gigs and waited for the word to get out, or come up with a "plan." The plan he used was to book the act into the first gig that he could get in the nearest big city (in this case it was Chicago). After this show was done, he rented the biggest hall in their home town and hired the current number one local band to back them up (no cash, just a split gate). He then took out big ads in the local paper, billing the act as "back from their successful Chicago appearance" with pictures and their name in huge type. At the bottom of the ad was, "opening the show will be our own "Those Guys." All of this cost him about two hundred bucks, and since the gig was successful, he made money. But the big thing was that he totally psyched out the town into accepting his band as the number one group. It was small-time, to be sure, but it worked.

On a bigger level is the story of another manager who wanted to pitch his act to record labels, but wanted to do it in a dramatic way that would make them sit up and take notice. Since this was a few years ago, there wasn't much video stuff around, and he used this to his advantage. Instead of playing a tape and then trying to get the label to come to a showcase, he rented some equipment and recorded a great "video demo." Without telling the label what he was planning, he walked into the appointment and set up all this equipment, including a large screen. Since he had made sure the video was a powerful performance, he only had to sit back and smile while the record execs fell all over themselves to sign the band (Don't try this trick now and expect it to have the same effect, because it has been done about eighty times since then). The idea is to come up with something new and use a creative approach to solving your business, as well as your musical problems.

## The Deal

From the day you get that cheap department store guitar to the time you're sitting in the A&R Director's office preparing to sign a contract, "getting a deal" will never be too far from your mind. It's what every artist is working to obtain. Of course, "the" deal may be with an important manager, agent, or producer instead of a record company, but it is still the thing that separates an amateur hustler from a star on the rise. You know you've got what it takes, but the rest of the world may not share that opinion until they see it in black and white ("Ajax Records has this day decreed that Tommy Dingbat has the makings of a bonified star").

There are no standard deals, so stop trying to find out about them. A deal means you got what you could get and they gave what they would give. It won't jeopardize your position if you ask for too much. The other person in the deal will just say no. If you ask for too little, however, they will just say yes (and that can be rather painful, especially if you find out that an act the label was less interested in got twice the money). You have to remember when negotiating a deal that the more you get, the more the label (or whoever) will follow through, because they want to get their money back. If you sign for fifty grand to do an album, and the "Gay Lumberjacks" sign for a hundred, whose record do you think the label will push the most? After a deal is signed, the record company's constant aim is recouping that investment. This is why, after you have your music and your show together, you must get some decent representation. Before you start negotiating with a label, you need a good manager or a hot shot attorney in there with you so that you don't screw yourself ("Sure thing, Mr. A&R Man, we'd be happy to pay the recording costs and have you reimburse us if it sells").

Another reason you want help when it comes time to deal with record companies is that there are certain ways to approach a label, which professionals have mastered and you have not. You don't ask an A&R man if you're good, for example. You're supposed to *know* you are good before you waste anyone's time. You have to act like you are already "there" without being a snob. People who negotiate deals with record companies are masters at acting as if they could care less if the label bites because there are others ready, willing, and able to sign the act. They always approach the label as if they were doing *them* a favor. They could go elsewhere, but "why not go with people who I know will appreciate a good act when they hear one."

It's as though they felt they owed it to the label to give them a chance at the act.

Acting out this little charade may sound idiotic and pretentious to you, but when it is done by a master dealmaker who is aware of all the subtle nuances of his craft, it works. Not only does it work, but it means literally thousands of extra dollars in the kitty. You have to approach a record label with an attitude that says "this is what I have, do you like it, or shall I take it somewhere else?" If the A & R guy starts picking it apart, ask for your tape back, because you don't want to waste anybody's time, especially yours. The question is not whether or not you have something good, but whether or not the A & R person will recognize it. I don't mean that you should bust into the office like Atilla The Hun and give the guy two minutes to cut you a check. I just mean you have to be confident of your material. If you have any doubts about it, don't even go until you've gotten rid of them.

At the risk of being redundant (so sue me if you're bored) let me remind you that you shouldn't waste time seeing an A & R man until you're ready. Remember that time is money and if you spin your wheels too often, the rubber will never touch the ground and you will never move forward.

When you make a deal with a record company, you want to get the money to record an album, a guarantee that even more money will be spent on promoting the album (twice as much if possible), and some extra cash for yourself. It is also ideal to get tour support so that the record label will pick up the tab while you travel around promoting the album at various clubs and concerts. It's a guarantee so that, if the gigs don't earn enough to support the tour, you won't go into the hole. The number of possible deals with their various clauses and financial figures is endless, and that is another reason why you need help to secure a good one. Get a professional to negotiate for you.

## Getting Screwed

Recognize that at some point in your career you are going to get screwed. Accept it as a matter of course and don't be paranoid (don't be stupid either). The only way you're going to get any experience is to get out there and do it. Essentially, getting screwed is making a bad deal. Everybody makes mistakes, but the biggest mistake is being stagnant because you're afraid you'll make a bad deal. Weigh every possible deal with its alternative. If the alternative to signing for less money than you would like is showcasing in your apartment, maybe you should take the offer. You've heard of Murphy's law that says "if something can go wrong, it will" (Murphy, by the way, was a famous concert promoter who always staged outdoor gigs in the Philippines during the monsoon season). Murphy's law is a bit too negative for my liking, but it is true that there are going to be decisions in your career that you will wish you could make again. So what? It's a risk you must take.

The idea is to learn how not to let a bad decision ruin you for life. That all depends upon your personal inner strength. There are going to be people who will intentionally screw you or, just as devastating, cop out on you when you need them most. Once you learn to focus on reality, establish and follow a plan for success, and believe in yourself; how well you handle your mistakes is the final key to success. Regard mistakes as learning experiences that everyone goes through. Pick yourself up and keep going.

How bad you get screwed not only has to do with how quick you recover from it, but how fast you realize that you have made a mistake. You've got to recognize when you are in a "can't win" situation. If it takes you five years to figure out that your manager isn't doing anything, you're as much to blame as he is for all the wasted time. You could have made that decision in six months and it would have been worth six months as a learning experience.

The reason people don't realize that they are in a bad deal is that they either don't make their expectations clear or they are afraid to admit they aren't happening. You should write out what you expect to happen from any deal. It's not something that can be put into a contract, but it's something that *must* at least be verbally understood. And since people tend to forget conversations, you should put it down on paper. What do you expect, and when do you expect it? Be realistic and try to get the person you are dealing with to agree on the projections. Make sure he has a copy of them and feels they are reasonable. It should be understood that communication is expected whenever an expectation is not met. This will help to keep your relationship with the person a working one which doesn't allow for unspoken resentments and doubts to create a gap in your understanding.

You also need such a list for yourself so that you can check out the progress of your relationship. Expectations tend to get foggy if they're not written down. Time drags on and things keep getting in the way which you view on a day to day basis, but pretty soon you wake up to the fact that you are going nowhere fast. This is just focusing on old reality again. I know you've heard it before, but I'm trying to teach you all the ways you can apply it. When a couple of things don't go according to your expectations, there's no cause for alarm, but if after six months, you're still waiting for things you thought would happen the week after you signed the deal, something is wrong. If you can agree on a list of expectations with your manager, for example, it will help insure a good consistent communication. It can even help affect an amiable parting when, after considerable time, you both realize that it just isn't happening the way you thought it would.

An incredible amount of valuable time is wasted because people are waiting on other people to come through for them. Don't put all your eggs in one guitar case (I hate cliches unless I can mess with them a bit). There is nothing more frustrating than to sit and wait on a manager for six months. Maybe you can't rush right down to the major labels and do your own talking, but there are other things you can do to further your career. People in these waiting situations often get the weird idea that if they do anything other than wait around, it is admitting they've lost hope in the thing they are waiting on. That's crazy! You've got to keep moving in this business. I have a friend who was waiting on his manager to line up some gigs. Nothing was happening, and he is a very active guy, so he was starting to go a little crazy. He was also broke, and one day he came up with a plan to relieve both his anxiety and financial need. Before he hooked up with his manager, he had a thousand singles pressed out of his demo tape (against my advice, I might add). He still had about four hundred of these babies sitting around the house, so he decided he would try to sell them. For the next five days he stood outside the supermarket and sold records to passers by. It sounds pretty crazy, you say? Well, he sold all four hundred records for fifty cents apiece. He made two hundred bucks and got his record into *four hundred* homes, just because he wasn't content to sit around and do nothing. He may become the only person in history to get a gold record by selling them on the street.

You don't have to be that extreme, but use your time for something more than worrying about what's happening with your manager. Some guys get up and make one phone call to their manager each day, and that's all they do for their career that day. You've got to practice and you've got to keep plugging. Don't do anything that would blow your gig with your manager or attorney or whatever, but keep active.

If you find yourself in a contract that is not doing you any good, get out of it. There is no such thing as a binding contract. Attorneys know that better than anyone, even though they make a fortune writing the things. Any contract can be broken if you want to break it badly enough. The worst that can happen is that you have to give up a small piece of the action to the person with whom you had the contract. Even that is better than wasting away. Having ninety percent of something is better than a hundred percent of nothing. With a good attorney, you may find that your contract has been violated, and not have to pay anything to get out of it except attorney's fees. By the way, have all your contracts examined by an attorney, and have your contracts with an attorney looked over by *another* attorney.

Getting screwed is most often having a potentially good deal turn sour. Often people feel that they are being screwed, but it may just be that the deal is over. The usefulness of the relationship has worn out. Time is not a factor. Sometimes a relationship wears out its usefulness in two weeks. You should try to look at things as falling through without blaming anybody. Blame causes resentment and resentment eats you up inside. You can't look at everything that goes wrong in life as "getting screwed." It can't always be "them" and not *you* who is wrong. Maybe a manager gave you some false expectations which he was unable to fulfill. It probably wasn't intentional because, after all, he wanted to make money off of the deal too. Maybe it was also partly your fault in the sense that the great songs you both thought you could write turned out not to be as great as they seemed.

What I'm saying is that fault is not the issue here. The issue is whether or not the deal is working, not whose fault it is that it failed. It's not who you can blame, but how you can go forward. You can't put in your resumé that "it was this guy's fault that I didn't do anything for three years." Nobody cares why you haven't happened yet except you, so don't tell them about it. If pouring out your sorrows makes you feel better, tell your best friend, and not your new manager. Telling a new manager that you were screwed by the last one only makes him doubt you.

Realize that you will be screwed and don't be afraid of it. Recognize when you've made a mistake and *move on*. Keep aware of your expectations so that you will know when a good deal has gone sour and don't put a lot of energy into blaming anyone. These things won't protect you from getting screwed, but they will keep you from screwing yourself.

# Chapter 12
# Where Do I Go From Here?

*"If you think of us next time, remember, our silence is a silence of love and not of indifference. Remember, we are writing in the sky instead of on paper—that's our song."*
                                                  **—John Lennon**\*

## Applying What You've Learned

Obviously, you are dedicated enough to making it in the music business to get through this book. Now the question is, are you dedicated enough to apply it to your life? I've read a lot of books and then tossed them up on the shelf thinking they were pretty good, and I was better off because of all the knowledge I had gained from reading them. Gaining knowledge is great, but applying it is much better.

Unless you've been taking meticulous notes as you've been reading, you need to go back and review some of the sections. As you review, concentrate on putting it into practice. Have you written out your goals yet? Have you formulated your plan for success, including the primary, secondary, and working goals?

\* *"A Love Letter From John And Yoko"* © *Spirit Music '79 reprinted in Rock-Pop, 6/17/79*

I'll bet this was all stuff that you planned on doing later, and now that you're almost done with the book, you are planning on waiting a little while longer. Hopefully, by then you will forget and can go back to *pretending* you are making it in music, instead of really doing it. Pretending is a lot more fun, isn't it? Well, I'm sorry, but I can't let you off that easily.

We've both wasted a lot of time and you've wasted some dough if you don't put this stuff into practice. I want you to get something out of this besides a good time (if you haven't had a good time, then reread the book and laugh at all my jokes). It won't take much longer for you to pencil out a plan and jot down some important points. Go step by step. When you've attained one goal, move on to the next. When you get into the studio, reread that section and take a few notes. When you're talking to managers, look for the things I've outlined. It's all pretty simple when you take it a rung at a time.

Before you can do anything though, you must formulate that plan for success. Use the one I've given you in this book (getting serious + putting a show together + writing the tunes + cutting a demo + getting a manager + making a deal + cutting an album + keeping your cool), or make up your own, but *have one*. And follow it.

## Believe In Yourself

The greatest source of direction you can have is your own gut feeling. But, before you can follow it, you must learn to recognize it, and that means separating it from fear and ego. Don't do things to stroke your ego, and don't do them because you're afraid. Once you've developed this inner confidence, you'll be rolling. When something inside tells you it's right, go for it. When the feeling says it's wrong, hold back and check it out a little longer. The more experience you get in making decisions, the easier it will get. Most people don't make decisions, they just let them happen. You want to be aware of your decisions because you want to know when you made the right ones and when you blew it. Keeping aware of this is how you develop the voice of experience.

If you're serious about any career, you must learn to believe in yourself. You can have doubts about the music business, but not about your own talent. Are you a good songwriter? If you can answer an unequivocal yes, then finding the right publisher is only a matter of effort. The biggest curve that others can throw you is causing you to doubt your own talent. And there are those who enjoy doing just that. Frank Sinatra sang, "Some people get their kicks out of stomping on a dream." Don't let them get to you.

### Believe In Your Team

Your team is the people who work with you on your career. If you're a songwriter, your team is your collaborator, your publisher, and maybe your manager and attorney. If you're a singer, it's your band, your writers, your agent, your record company, and your manager and attorney. You've got to believe in these people. If you don't, why are you working with them? Clear up the doubts or get out of the relationship. If you're afraid of your manager, you've got problems. I don't care how much intimidation is part of his technique. If you can't call him up and ask why he isn't doing anything for your act, or tell him that you don't feel things are progressing quite fast enough, then you don't need him. You don't need the anxiety.

There are a lot of people out there who can help you. It only takes one to make the difference between success and donuts for dinner. One good contact who really believes in your talent can help you immensely. So, if you're not happy with the people on your team, go to the people store and pick out some new ones. It's almost that simple. Just because you are dealing with individuals, doesn't mean you can't amicably break off relationships and seek out people more suited or more committed to your career.

When something first starts happening in your career on an important level, there is a tendency not to look too closely at it, (the old gift horse routine). If you can't be objective about a development in your career, ask someone you trust to help you. Fearing that you might jeopardize the situation can cause you not to ask the necessary questions. If a relationship is so delicate it can't withstand communication, then it isn't the right relationship.

Don't con yourself into believing that someone is fulfilling a role in your life when they are not. Don't pretend that you have a manager who is really out there hustling for you, when you can't even get him on the phone. It is this kind of thing that keeps most artists from finding the *right* team. *Pretending* you have the right people working with you keeps you from *finding* the right ones. The team concept is built on trust and talent. If either is missing, it becomes a disadvantage instead of an advantage. No one person can do it all on his own, and no one can do it with the wrong people helping them. Believe in your team or get a team you can believe in.

## The Ladder

Take it one rung at a time. Make sure you do it right before you move on, and you won't have to go backwards. Make sure your band can keep time before you look for a producer. Remember that the more things you do well in the beginning, the easier it will be in the home stretch. *Take your time.*

Another aspect of the ladder is that no matter how fast you go up, the trip down is even faster. And as you go down, you invariably pass those people you stepped on as you climbed "to the top." If you think using people and throwing them away when you're done, like last night's supper, is the way to get ahead, you should realize that you may have to face those folks again. And it's usually when you need them the most, on the way back down the ladder. Don't be too ruthless on your way up unless you want to be treated ruthlessly on the way down.

Everybody will love you when you're a star, but the moment your sales start slipping, some of these new found "friends" will start disappearing as well. When it gets real bad, the people you once used will be using you and saying things like "see schmuck, who needs you?" Pop music is a notoriously fickle business, and staying on top depends on consistently doing the basic elements of stage, records, and business, correctly. There are a lot of ex-rock stars who are now cheese salesmen in Wisconsin.

In the beginning you fight to be a star, and then you fight to collect your money. Another reason you need good representation is to help you collect your dough. Record companies can be very slow in paying out royalties sometimes, and "unusual" expenses have a way of popping up. The best way to make sure the record company is going to pay you everything they promised is to have them believe that you can still make a lot more money for them. People who have flash-in-the-pan hits sometimes have a lot of trouble. One hit and they're obsolete. The record company has no use for them anymore and they may be very slow in paying them. Hopefully, they will collect their money before their career is totally over. A lot of these guys wind up taking a merry-go-round ride in the music business. This happens most to those artists who ego out when they score big. All of a sudden they're telling everybody what to do. The people who would have helped them are turned off, and the guys who busted their buns to make their record sell the last time, suddenly could care less. The result is that the artist flops, and everyone is glad to see him do it. No doubt he has also alienated the label with his "star" attitude and they respond by slowing down the royalty checks. So now he's broke and back at the bottom where he started. Only now he is in a worse position because he has a lot of enemies in the business.

You have to learn to be tactful if you want a long career. You can't push people around and not expect them to push back. When you're "Mr. Big-Time" it's hard to imagine that anything can go wrong, but if you alienate enough people, sooner or later the balloon will burst. Step on a lot of little folks on your way to the top and they will get you in the end. This business is crazy and you need some real friends to help you survive in it. Don't sell them down the river. Maybe you are fantastic on stage and you can write great tunes every day if you want to, so you're not worried. Still, if you want to be around for a long time, you need guys who will push extra hard on that one record that doesn't quite match up to the others. A real "star" can slip once in a while and the love and effort of those around him will pick up the slack. But, let a conniving balloon-headed egotist make one mistake and the rest of the world is too busy applauding to care how far he falls.

So while you're hustling up the ladder of success, remember to make allies instead of enemies. Realize that some day you might fall and it will be a lot easier if there are a few people there to catch you when you do.

## Fear & Greed

Isn't it nice that I let you read a whole book about making it in the music business and then tell you that you're in store for a lot of trouble at the top? I don't mean to paint such a bleak picture, but I do want to warn you about certain things. Fear and greed are two of them. They are your biggest enemies in the music business. You have to watch out for them in yourself and in others. If you're not able to control your fears, you'll never pass an audition. In fact, you'll never be able to make a serious attempt at anything because you will always be giving in to that voice that says "give up, you can't win." Putting together a band, playing gigs, recording a demo, and playing your tape for managers and agents, are all situations which require you to overcome fear. If you give in to fear at a two-bit level, how do you think you are going to feel when it's time to play in front of twenty-thousand poeple? Oh, you think that by then you will be a "professional" and it won't be a problem. Well, how are you going to become a professional if you're afraid to ask the kid across the street to join your band? By taking it a step at a time.

Learn to recognize when you're afraid, instead of disguising it as something else. Sometimes saying things like "I don't think the guy is good enough to be in our band" or "we don't want to play there anyway" is just giving in to fear. Make a resolution that you are not going to make choices based on fear. Caution and good sense, maybe, but not fear. It might be more difficult for you to admit all these fears that normally would be rationalized away as something else, but after a while it will get easier. And you'll be amazed at how much you learn once you start making real decisions.

You also have to watch out for the fears of others. Every band seems to have one guy who is scared to move. The sooner you help him realize and overcome his problem, the faster your band will move down the road. Detecting fear in others is not always that easy because it is covered up with other things like anger or apathy. Sometimes if you come on too strong, people will shy away because your energy and enthusiasm scares them. From the old lady on the Park Board who is afraid to rent you the auditorium, to the hot-shot Hollywood manager who is afraid to admit his career is over, you have to guard against the fears of others from slowing you down. Often, there isn't much you can do about it, but sometimes being aware of it is enough.

Greed also strikes at all levels of the music business. In the beginning it might be something like whether or not the five hours of hard labor spent by your roadie to set up the equipment is really worth ten dollars. Later on it's looking at the trusted agent who brought you from the Hootsville Bowling Alley to the Hollywood Bowl and thinking "we could be making more money if we didn't have to pay him." It's the same game.

You have to recognize who is doing what, and what it is worth. Don't just recognize it when you need it done, but remember it when you're paying out the money. I wish I had a nickel for all the salesmen who were promised a high commission rate until they started making "too much" money and management decided to lower their percentages. People are always worried about being taken advantage of, and most of the time that fear has something to do with greed or with its sister, selfishness. The music business is an industry of incredible wealth and power. If you "make it" in this business, there is almost no way you will not be rich (at least for a couple of weeks). Try not to get caught up in the greed that surrounds big money. Don't be so concerned about amassing more and more, without giving thought to the ethics of the situation. I know it's kind of hard to imagine yourself sitting behind the desk of a huge conglomerate someday, when at the moment you're wondering how to keep the lights on in your trailer, but you have to accept the responsibility of your goals. Being a rock star can mean unfathomable wealth and power and there is a certain responsibility which goes with that. I'm not trying to preach, but the fact of the matter is that, if you abuse the privilege of such wealth, you will either lose it or lose yourself to it. There isn't a whole lot of difference between slaving for some factory and being a slave to your own empire. When you are at the top, try to remember what it was like on the bottom, without getting scared. If you can do that, you can keep your life from centering around your wealth, power, or fame.

Fear usually hits you hardest on the way up, and greed is usually what brings you back down. Don't be scared of making it, and once you've made it, don't be scared of losing it. Being selfish won't get you there any faster, and being greedy won't help you keep it any longer. I assume your goal is not just being a famous and wealthy rock star, but being a *happy*, famous and wealthy rock star. Even if you just want to make a decent living from your musical or executive abilities, you still have to watch out for fear and greed. Never forget that they are your most dangerous enemies.

## Good Luck!

One last thing. Have a sense of humor about all of this. Take it serious enough to really make an effort to apply it to your life, but don't let it drag you down. You are in a business that is, by most standards, relatively crazy. It can be really nutso sometimes. You have to be able to laugh at yourself or you won't survive. You can't change the past and redo all your mistakes, so learn to laugh at them while resolving to do better next time. More things are going to go wrong than go right, so keeping your sense of humor can make the difference between success and failure or insanity. Did you ever wonder why so many rock stars go bananas or turn to heavy drugs? It's because they take themselves way too seriously. It's pretty hard to read how heavy you are in the pop mags and then laugh off your mistakes. It's especially difficult because everybody else takes you so seriously.

A lot of pop stars think their world is going to end when they wake up and find they don't like their own music anymore. If they hadn't become accustomed to being treated like the Egyptian Pharaohs, they would be able to deal more effectively with the problem. Once you start regarding your music as being sacred, it gets kind of difficult to accept the need for change. Being a successful recording artist is no different from being a successful anything else, but it *seems* different.

Don't get so caught up in yourself that the music becomes secondary to the "identity." Otherwise, the reason you wanted to be a success will get lost, and the enjoyment you derive from that success will disappear with it. Don't let the thing you love most become something you hate because you take it too seriously. Learn to back off and enjoy yourself. What's the point of selling a million records a year if you're miserable? Please don't wind up one of these guys who gaze out the window of their Beverly Hills mansion wishing they were hustling on the streets again.

Also realize that some day it is all going to come to an end. Don't be shocked when it's over. Pop music is not the most endurable of careers, and while you're doin it, you might give some thought to what you want to do when you're fifty (old men in tight leather pants just don't make it). Don't ruin your career by always being afraid of what will happen when it ends. Enjoy it while it lasts and realize that you're not chained to it. There are other things you can do, and other things you can enjoy. All you have to do is open up to them. But, accept from the start that you won't be doing this forever. Everything comes to an end.

I told you in the beginning and I'm telling you now—this is a tough business. If you really want it, you can have it, as long as you don't give up and don't let it destroy you as a human being. There's a lot of people doing it, but you've got a jump on them. You've got a plan and you can separate the reality from the fantasy. Remember that your key to success is in that last sentence. Try to become a success on the inside as well as on the outside and keep your sense of humor. Good luck, and don't forget me when you're on top.

# APPENDIX 1
## THE STATE OF THE RECORD BUSINESS
## UPDATED EDITION

During the time since this book was originally published, the music business has undergone a tremendous sales slump. This situation intensifies the necessity for those within it to be objective and focus on the reality rather than individual fantasies. You may not see how a sales slump can affect someone in an "aspiring" situation when the odds of success are something like one out of a thousand in the first place, but a serious recession affects the entire industry. Looking at the causes of this slump can help your perspective of the music business, so I've included this section in the revised edition.

For a long time, the record business believed it was somewhat immune to the economic wars of the world. This belief was based on the axiom that in hard times people still find the bucks for those things that provide them with a much needed escape from their problems. The axiom may still be true, but it does have its limits. For one reason, there are other products that provide an even better escape for some people than listening to music. One legal example would be video games. An illegal example would be marijuana. In any case, the "escape" axiom alone is not enough to insure the safety of an industry with structural and technological problems as severe as the music business.

On the technological side, it is now as easy to steal an album as it is to buy it. The Warner Communications Inc. (WCI) Report on Home Taping published in March of 1982 concluded that $609 million was spent on blank audio tape during 1980 for the purpose of recording music or other professional entertainment. This translated into $2.85 billion of lost sales to the recording industry, according to the survey. It can be argued forever whether this represents a fifteen to fifty percent loss to the industry but there is no doubt that it is a sizable chunk. If this isn't enough, the rent-a-record mania spreading through countries like Japan and Sweden holds another ax over our heads, and in Southern California the state is trying to collect a retroactive sales tax (Billboard, Feb. 27, 82). Nothing like citing an entire industry on tax evasion to beef up the state coffers.

Out and out piracy also is still choking profits. It has been estimated that more than 25% of the records out there are fakes (Billboard Feb. 6, 82). They look the same, but they are bootlegged and then packaged as close as possible to the real thing. These records are often offered to the retail stores or distributors at a tremendous discount because the pirates are paying no royalties, no recording costs, and no advertising or promotion expenses. Over eighty huge pirate pressing plants are said to be in Singapore alone. Tremendous strides have been made in passing and enforcing piracy laws, but the amount of international red tape is unbelievable.

So roughly half of our industry is being lost to dishonesty, whether it be on the level of high school taping parties or colossal pirating operations. The solutions to these rip-offs are many and varied, and unfortunately are still in the discussion stages. A tax on blank tape which is then equally distributed to the music industry is one remedy to the loss of income through home taping. An electronic tone that magically appears upon attempted reproduction is another. Some of the experts believe that, in the future, digital discs will solve some of these problems because both records and tapes would become obsolete by comparison of sound quality and durability. As of this writing, nothing can be clearly decided. It is interesting to note in relation to home taping, however, that, according to the WCI survey, only 25% taped at home "so that they didn't have to buy the album." The rest gave reasons as diverse as "home taping was fun" and "it preserved or gave better quality than the records and tapes available in the stores." In other words, while we still don't have a total answer, we should recognize that some of the causes, like quality, are within our control.

There was a time when we could have controlled these problems much easier if we had devoted more attention to them. It doesn't exactly take a rocket scientist to figure out that millions of high quality home taping units could add up to a problem for the record business. The reason dollars and attention weren't given to the problem before it became a monster is that the industry didn't care, as long as it was prospering. Everybody was too busy raking it in during the golden years to put enough effort into research. This is an example of the structural problems of our industry.

You must remember that the record business is a comparatively young industry which still has many structural bugs to work out. For example, it has only been in recent years that record companies stopped allowing distributors a full money back guarantee if the product didn't sell. Stores could return records at any time and receive full credit. This policy led to the dubious practice of "shipping gold or platinum" and sometimes eating over half the product in returns rather than shipping as needed, even if it didn't cause as much of a sensation. Hype doesn't work when everybody is doing it, and our industry is so steeped in hype that we must do a serious appraisal.

There is a lack of openness in our industry. One of the reasons it has been difficult to tackle problems such as piracy or home duplicating is that nobody wants to be totally open about their figures, which makes it pretty hard to even assess the situation, much less determine the solution. Competition prevents a wide open policy of course, but sometimes a lack of information leads to red tape and hidden administrative costs. An example of this is the time-consuming and roundabout method that A&R departments use to deal with the huge volume of unprofessional tapes that pour into their offices. This could be minimized to some degree by taking a realistic approach and informing the public. Most people are not going to bother sending in a noisy cassette they made on their economy model portable if they know that this type of thing really doesn't have much of a chance. In the music industry, we sometimes have executives who realistically do nothing but screen people and tapes away from the next rung on the ladder. This kind of thing exists in every business, but we've really let it get out of hand.

A more serious problem is sort of skitzoid inverse of "The Peter Principle". When you have tremendous industry growth, two things that happen are big corporations get into the game and things like "what to do with all the money so that the government doesn't get it" become important. Both elements produce accountants like they were rabbits coming out of a hat. The accountants do their job and "streamline" things so that phrases like "cost-efficient" are suddenly right up there with phrases like "in the grooves". This process leads rather quickly to the short term profit game. Big money means stocks, and that means looking good year by year. The guys making the decisions have to explain why if they don't produce yearly growth. This can sometimes lead to making decisions which are "good for everybody" on the short term and suicidal in the long run The tragic part is that sometimes the guys that play best with the figures know the crash will have to hit, but they're more worried about keeping up the payments on the Porsche and their wife's face lift.

This nightmare is what gives unnatural life to elements like disco. Disco was a form of popular music like many others but it got out of hand because it was a natural for producing short term profits. Point number one is that disco didn't require name artists. In fact, disco was more of a producers' phenomenon than an artist's passion. It had a sort of formula which actually got to the point of measuring the B.P.M.'s (beats per minute) of the bass drum to see that it held a steady 120. You don't need a Bob Dylan for that. There were some great disco records and a lot of great artists recorded disco, but the climate of the industry forced many of them into it.

Disco sold like crazy, so everybody cranked it out and force-fed the fad as much as possible. That's all fine and dandy, but the real record dogs that built this industry knew the traditional life blood of the music business was in establishing new artists. Real live artists that could go on a stage and sing and keep turning out consistent quality. Not people with names like "The Aquarious Brothers" who could only do exactly what the producer told them to do one time in the studio, and then hire some pretty backup singers and forty-three studio cats to go on the road, and at best capture half of the record with none of the feeling. In any business when the average quality goes down for a substantial period of time, serious repercussions are soon to follow.

Part of the problem is that music quality didn't seem to matter anymore. It if got played, it sold, and if it sold, it made dough. We became an industry with two products: little records with big holes, and big records with little holes. We sold more and more records, and the quality of them seemed to become less and less important. Maybe it wasn't our fault, but there's no denying that some form of greed caught up to us.

The other element that the accountants kept forgetting during the disco era is that all fads get old unless they evolve. And when they get old, everybody hates them. The guys that put disco down the worst, now are the guys that beat their brains out all over their satin suits dancing to it at the Happy Feet Lounge only a short time ago. They are the same guys who are wearing the dry-cleaned cowboy suits around now until somebody tells them that train has passed as well. So suddenly everybody hated disco, and there were very few new heroes to take its place on the charts.

So you think a whole rush of new talent would bust in, right? Wrong. During the financial boom, the guys that played those kind of games the best took the power and a lot of the jobs. So we had things like formula A&R, where you spread a million dollars over ten acts and more or less throw them up against a wall, knowing that a few of them will stick and pay for all the rest. This kind of thing actually works during a boom market. Once the recessive market hit, however, all these financial formulas and policies choked business even further.

During the boom years, the giants of this industry kept growing and made a regular habit of swallowing up anything which looked even remotely promising. There were fewer and fewer companies to deal with, and that meant the structure was getting tighter and tighter until the crash hit. As is so often the case with industry, economic difficulty produced new success stories. When the crunch slowed down the big labels, the small labels began to bloom. New companies sprang up, staffed by seasoned old pros and unbrainwashed upstarts and many of them experienced tremendous growth. The industry giants are like the Spanish Armada, chained by their very size into policies and politics that prevent their adapting to the current market, while the small labels navigate the swift economic currents more freely.

The success formula that has helped so many of these small labels prosper is the same one that built the record business. Really discovering and promoting talent is something of a lost art to much of the industry, but it's being resurrected. Thus, the cycle of creative people producing success, success leading to uncreative people in control, and ultimate problems has returned to its roots. The big corporate giants can no longer ignore the situation and are responding. The video revolution, new sound technology and better business practices are leading our industry into an exciting era. In a very real sense, this is a great time to be in the record business because it is being redefined and hopefully better structured to handle its growth.

It's growing up!

# GLOSSARY

(some hip and semi-hip terms you can throw around at parties)

**A & R**—Artist & Repertoire, the department of a record company that is responsible for signing artists and "assisting" them creatively in such things as the selection of a producer and song material.

**Airplay**—time on the radio. Airplay sells records.

**Baffle**—big fat portable walls of mush that suck up sound in a recording studio.

**Basic Track**—the foundation of a record usually consisting of the drums, bass, and rhythm instruments.

**Bullet**—a footnote added to a chart position to indicate fast upward movement.

**Chartbuster**—hit record that "busts through the top of the charts."

**Chops**—a meat dish usually made of pork or lamb. Also a technical ability that comes with practice or use. A musician who "keeps his chops up" either practices a lot or wears pork chops on his head.

**Clicktrack**—metronome like device to aid timing or rhythm that is heard through headphones during a recording session.

**Clout**—power, connections, the ability to get things done and to make deals.

**Commercial**—saleable, likely to get played on the radio, possessing qualities similar to other hits.

**Crossover**—a record originally promoted in one market which "crosses over" to be a hit in another market. A country record may crossover to the pop market for example.

**Demo**—a tape done for demonstration purposes usually to try to secure a record, publishing, or management deal.

**Downtime**—time when work is halted in a recording session due to equipment malfunction or time when a studio has not been booked for use.

**Dud**—a record that flops. Also, a person who flops.

**Ears**—the ability to recognize a hit song or act after only a few listenings.

**Fader**—control on a studio console which regulates input or output of sound level.

**Gig**—job, especially a club or concert performance.

**Gold Record**—award presented for sales in excess of one million singles or 500,000 albums.

**Grammy**—music industry award presented by the NARAS (National Association of Recording Arts and Sciences).

**Headphone Mix**—an alcoholic beverage made with ¼" recording tape, guitar strings, and melted rubber from old headphones. Also, the blend of sounds heard through the headphones in a recording session.

**Hook**—a musical or lyrical phrase that stands out and is easily remembered.

**Hype**—publicity used to feed the promotional machines of the music business. Hype may or may not be true, but it should be "sensational."

**Image**—the public's impression of an artist or product.

**Master**—a tape recording done for release as a record.

**Mechanicals**—song royalties paid from the sales of records.

**Mix**—blend of sounds. The mix is particularly important in multi-track recording.

**Monster**—smasherino, a huge hit record.

**MOR**—Middle Of The Road, Easy Listening Music, softer and slower than rock. Barry Manilow is an MOR artist.

**Multi-track recording**—recording a multiplicity of audio tracks on magnetic tape which allows you to isolate sounds and record them at different times.

**Overdub**—in multi-track recording, any element that is added after the basic track.

**Panning**—the movement of sound from right to left or left to right.

**Ping-pong**—tennis for wimps, also the mixing down of two or more tracks onto a lesser amount of tracks.

**Platinum Record**—award for sales in excess of one million albums.

**Points**—a percentage, usually of the profit of a record.

**Pot**—studio console control similar to a fader. Pot is often used in the studio.

**Prima-donna**—conceited individual.

**Production fee**—fee paid to the producer of a record.

**Punch-in & Punch-out**—a method of correcting mistakes on on multi-track tape by punching in the correction at the right time and punching out before erasing valid material.

**Recovery Time**—time spent drowning one's sorrows or avoiding reality after a disappointment before new progress is attempted. Recovery Time is the great time waster in the music business.

**Rhythm Machine**—mechanical device which "plays" various rhythm patterns as selected.

**Riff**—a particular group of notes.

**Roadie**—person in the employ of a musical act who is usually responsible for moving and setting up sound equipment.

**Royalty Period**—the time in which royalties are computed and paid to artists, producers, and publishers (usually every six months or quarterly).

**Sel-Sync**—tape machines equipped with Sel-Sync allow you to both record and listen to what is being recorded without a time lag.

**Spec time**—free recording time given to an act on the speculation that they will secure a deal and reimburse the studio.

**Studio musicians**—musicians who hire out their services for recording sessions. Have guitar, will travel.

**Tip sheets**—newsletters or magazines that are specifically designed to meet the programming needs of radio stations.

**Trades**—magazines that report in-depth on the music industry.

**Tracking**—recording basic tracks.

**Vamp**—a seductive woman, also an ending to a song that repeats over and over while gradually fading to silence.

**Zepulate**—a word I made up to end the glossary. It has to do with making love and listening to Led Zeppelin records at the same time.

# What Educators are Saying

"I enjoyed The Platinum Rainbow. It brings the reader to the inside of the entertainment fields, expecially the do and do nots of the recording industry."
—Dr. Paul O.W. Tanner, *Music Dept., UCLA*

"The Platinum Rainbow, is the finest book of its kind published to date. It is informative, but never dry. The subtle sense of humor marvellously enhances the message the book tries to get across. This book has hit the market dead center."
—Joel Leach, *California State University. Northridge, CA.*
*Past Pres. NAJE*

"Informative, authoritative and enjoyable. We will be using it as a resource in our readings course in "The Business of Music." Thanks for such a beautiful experience."
—K. Newell Dayley, *Chairman, Music Performance,*
*Brigham Young University, Provo, Utah*

"At Musicians Institute we try to present a curriculum where the aesthetics of music is balanced with the business of getting into and staying in the music business. That is why The Platinum Rainbow is recommended reading for all our students."
—Pat Hicks, President

"This is the book we've always wanted. A practical, valuable, honest, funny, and easy-to-read resource. Required reading for everyone even remotely interested in pursuing a music industry career...takes years off the "school of hard knocks" curriculum."
—John Braheny, *Co-founder/Director, Los Angeles*
*Songwriters Showcase*

"The Platinum Rainbow seminar was realistically structured to capture the attention of and help, by it's pertinent topics, the students who are striving to enter some aspect of the commercial music business. Your ability to be sincere and honest and your stimulating, informed guest speakers captured the interest and motivated the students. "
—Priscilla Remeta, *Chairman, Music Dept., Long Beach City*
*College, California*

# What Radio is Saying

"The Platinum Rainbow *really* does tell you how to succeed in the music business without selling you soul."
—Sonny Melendrez. *KFI Los Angeles*

"Written by insiders. The Platinum Rainbow lays is out the way 'it is' rather than the way we'd 'like it to be.' The directories of producers. agents. record companies. etc. are also invaluable."
—Michael Benner, *KLOS Los Angeles*

"The phone response from the burgeoning musicians out there and artists who are trying to get discovered attests to the tremedous popularity of the book."
—Eric Tracy. *America Overnight*

"The praises have been sung by everyone and I agree. One of the most honest approaches I have seen."
Dave Benson. *WMET-FM Chicago*

"If you have any interest at all in the music business you ought to see this book because it is certainly a bible of truth."
—Tom Webb. *WLUP Chicago*

"I wish I had had a book like this when I started out in music.
—Steve King *WIND Chicago*

"A unique book because it is real and honest."
—Don Hertzgarrd *WCCO Minneapolis*

"Somewhere over the rainbow God gave Monaco and Riordan the good sense to write a book about the pot at the end of the musical rainbow, and what may or may not be in it. I'm in the business of delivering information, this book helps when it comes to informing my audience about the crazy business of making music."
—Pat Powers *KDKB Phoenix*

"The adjective that best describes this book, is realistic. I read it with great interest."
—Jackie Runice, *WLS-FM Chicago*

"It's great to see two successful people in the music business share so many industry secrets. It was a bold move. Knowing how difficult it is to get a hit record, I wouldn't want to try it without The Platinum Rainbow."
—Preston Westmoreland *KTAR Phoenix*

"Intimately knowledgeable about the music business. It's superb."
—Dick Pomerantz *KSTP, Minneapolis*

"Everything you need to know about the music business and really everything that's fun to read about. It's imminently readable. I tell you, you won't be able to put it down."
—Paul Wallach *KIEV Glendale*

# APPENDIX 3
## STUDIOS/SCHOOLS
## OFFERING RECORDING COURSES
## IN THE U.S.

---

### ALABAMA

**BROADWAY SOUND STUDIO**
**UNIV. NORTH ALABAMA**
1307 Broadway St., Sheffield, 35660 (205)
381-1833.
**RECORDING INSTITUTE OF AMERICA**
**AT SOLID ROCK SOUND**
Recording studios, 536 Huffman Rd., Birmingham 35215. (205) 833-6906. Noah White.
**SAMFORD UNIV.**
800 Lakeshore Dr., Birmingham 37209. (205)
870-2011. Bob Burroughs.
**STUDIO FOUR**
PO Box 6572, Dothan 36302. (205) 794-9067.
Jerry Wise.
**UNIVERSITY OF NORTH ALABAMA**
Commercial Music Dept. Wesleyan Ave.,
Florence 35630. (205) 766-4100. Dr. James
Sempson.
**WOODRICH RECORDING STUDIOS**
George Wallace Park Dr., Lexington 35648.
(205) 229-5470, 247-3983. Wood Richardson

---

### CALIFORNIA

**ACCUSOUND RECORDING STUDIO**
4274-1/2 El Cajon Blvd., San Diego 92105.
(714) 281-6693. John Hildebrand.
**AYRE STUDIOS**
458 A Reynolds Circle, San Jose 95112. (408)
279-2973. Richard Nebel.
**BLUE BEAR SCHOOL OF MUSIC**
Bldg. D, Fort Mason Center, San Francisco,
CA 94123. (415) 673-3600. Steve Savage.
**BUSINESS ACADEMY OF MUSIC**
PO Box 794, Hollywood 90028. (213) 876-
2461. Martin G. Kugell, Director
**CAL STATE NORTHRIDGE**
Nordhoff, Northridge 91325. (213) 885-3700.
**COLLEGE FOR RECORDING ARTS**
665 Harrison St., San Francisco 94107. (415)
781-6306. Leo de Gar Kulka.
**ELECTRONIC SOUNDS**
PO Box 1251, Reseda 91335. (213) 726-8050
X 626. James Roberson.

**GOLDEN WEST COLLEGE, SCHOOL OF**
**THE RECORDING ARTS**
15744 Goldenwest St., Huntington Beach
92647. (714) 892-7711 Evan Williams.
**GRAMOPHONE STUDIOS**
13889 Meyer Rd., Whittier 90604. (213) 941-
6650. Dave Paton.
**DICK GROVE MUSIC WORKSHOPS**
12754 Ventura Blvd., Studio City 91604. (213)
985-0905 William Wolfe.
**HEAVENLY RECORDING STUDIOS**
**RECORDING TECHNIQUE SEMINARS**
1020 35th Ave., Sacramento 95822. (916)
428-5888 Steven G. Somers.
**HOLLYWOOD SCHOOL OF REC'G ARTS**
PO Box 9575. N. Hollywood, 91609. (213)
462-5775. Doc Siegel.
**INSTITUTE OF AUDIO/VIDEO ENG'G.**
1831 Hyperion Ave., Hollywood 90027. (213)
666-3003. Lydia E. Towner.
**INSTITUTE OF SOUND RECORDING**
3420 Camino Del Rio North Ste. 225, San
Diego 92108. (714) 281-7744. Aaron Berg
**KENDUN RECORDERS**
619 S. Glenwood Pl. Burbank 91506. (213)
843-8096. Leila Greenstone.
**LONG BEACH CITY COLLEGE**
Commercial Music Dept. 4901 E. Carson St.,
Long Beach 90808. (213) 420-9313. Priscilla
Remeta, Chairman; George Shaw, Commercial Music Coordinator; Tim Parsh, Recording Arts.
**MEDIA MASTERS INC.**
3015 Ocean Park Blvd., Santa Monica 90405.
(213) 450-2288. Melody Shepherd.
**MIX-MASTER RECORDING**
6881 Oakdale Rd., Winton 95388. (209) 358-
5744. Jim Schriber.
**MOORPARK COLLEGE**
Moorpark 93021. (805) 529-2321. Al Miller.
**ORANGE COAST COLLEGE**
2701 Fairview Rd., Costa Mesa 92626. (714)
556-5818/5629. Howard M. Judkins.
**RECORDING INSTITUTE OF AMERICA**
1519 S. Grand, Santa Ana 92705. (714) 547-
5466. Hank Quinn.
**RECORDING INSTITUTE OF AMERICA**
**AT NATURAL SOUND REC'G STUDIO**
9851 Prospect Ave., Santee 92071. (714) 448-
6000. Lou Mattazaro.

**SAN FRANCISCO CONSERVATORY OF MUSIC**
1201 Ortega St., San Francisco, 94122 (415) 564-8086.
**SAN FRANCISCO STATE UNIV.**
1600 Holloway, San Francisco 94132. (415) 469-1507. Paul Smith.
**SHERWOOD OAKS EXPERIMENTAL COLLEGE**
1445 N. Las Palmas Blvd., Hollywood 90028. (213) 462-0669. Gary Shusett.
**SOUND MASTER REC'G ENG. SCHOOLS**
10747 Magnolia Blvd., N. Hollywood 91601. (213) 650-8000. Barbara Ingoldsby.
**SOUNDTRAX ART OF REC'G SCHOOL**
8170-U Ronson Rd., San Diego 92111. (714) 560-8449.
**STUDIO ONE**
22920 Bay Ave., Edgemont 92508. (714) 653-2042. Jack Jackson.
**TRACK RECORD DEMO WORKSHOP**
5249 Melrose Ave., Los Angeles 90038. (213) 467-9432.
**TRES VIRGOS STUDIOS**
1925 Francisco Blvd., G. San Rafael, 94901. Robin Yeager.
**UNIVERSITY OF CALIFORNIA ARTS EXTENSION/UCLA**
10995 Le Conte Ave., Los Angeles 90024. (213) 825-9064. Note: Classes conducted at Hope St. Studio, 607 N. Ave. 64, Los Angeles 90042.
**UNIVERSITY OF SOUND ARTS**
6525 Sunset Blvd., Ste. G-7, Hollywood 90028. (213) 467-5256. Tracine Duncan.
**UNIVERSITY OF SOUTHERN CALIFORNIA**
Los Angeles 90007. (213) 741-2388.

## CANADA

**TREBAS INST. OF REC'G ARTS**
1 Place Ville Marie, Ste 3235, Montreal, Quebec, Canada H3B 3M7. (514) 842-3815. David P. Leonard.

## COLORADO

**COLORADO AUDIO INSTITUTE**
680 Indiana St., Golden 80401. (303) 279-2500. Bill Schereck.
**UNIVERSITY OF COLORADO AT DENVER SCHOOL OF MUSIC**
1100 14 St., Denver 80202. (303) 629-2727. Dr. Frantz L. Roehmann.
**CARIBOU RANCH**
Box 310, Nederland 80466. (303) 258-3215. (weekdays 9am-5pm) Steve Hebrock, Jerry Mahler.

## CONNECTICUT

**BUSINESS ACADEMY OF MUSIC**
PO Box 4026, Woodbridge 06525. (203) 735-5883 Martin G. Kugell
**R B Y RECORDING STUDIO**
Rd 1, Main St., Southbury 06488. (203) 264-3666. Marjorie Jones.
**RECORDING INSTITUTE OF AMERICA AT TROD NOSSEL RECORDING**
Box 57, 10 George St., Wallingford 06492. (203) 269-4465. Richard D. Robinson.
**UNIVERSITY OF BRIDGEPORT**
285 Park Ave., Bridgeport 06602. (203) 576-4016.
**UNIVERSITY OF HARTFORD**
200 Bloomfield Ave., Hartford 06117. (203) 243-4595.

## DISTRICT OF COLUMBIA

**CATHOLIC UNIVERSITY**
620 Michigan Ave., NE, Washington 20064. (202) 635-5000.

## FLORIDA

**FLORIDA STATE UNIVERSITY**
600 W. College Ave., Tallahassee 32306. (904) 644-2525.
**FLORIDA STATE UNIVERSITY SCHOOL OF MUSIC**
Tallahassee 32306. (904) 644-3424.
**RECORDING INSTITUTE OF AMERICA AT CYPRESS REC'G STUDIO INC.**
120 N. Fifth St., Jacksonville Beach 32250. (904) 246-8222. David T. Plummer.
**UNIVERSITY OF MIAMI SCHOOL OF MUSIC**
PO Box 248165, Coral Gables 33124. (304) 284-2433. Bill Porter.

## GEORGIA

**GEORGIA STATE UNIVERSITY COMMERCIAL DEPARTMENT**
University Plaza, Atlanta 30303. (404) 658-3513. Carter D. Thomas.
**THE SOUND ROOM INC.**
325 Patterson Ave., Fort Oglethorpe 30742. (404) 866-2432.

# HAWAII

**RECORDING INSTITUTE OF AMERICA
AT AUDISSEY**
679 Auahi St., Honolulu 96813 (808) 521-6791. Andria MacDonald.

# ILLINOIS

**ARTIST WORKSHOP RECORDING**
2228 E. Maple St., Kankakee 60901. (815) 933-7090. George Marakas.
**COLUMBIA COLLEGE**
600 S. Michigan Ave., Chicago 60605. (312) 663-1600. H. Thaine Lyman.
**CREATIVE AUDIO**
705 Western Ave., Urbana 61801. (217) 367-3530. Michael Reed.
**HEDDEN WEST RECORDERS**
1200 Remington Rd. Schaumburg, 60195. (312) 885-9330. Michael Freeman.
**ILLINOIS CENTRAL COLLEGE**
Rt. 24, East Peoria 61611. (309) 694-5011.
**WAUBONSEE COLLEGE**
Rt. 47 & Harter Rd., Sugar Grove 60554. (312) 466-4811.

# INDIANA

**BUTLER UNIVERSITY**
4600 Sunset Ave., Indianapolis 46208. (317) 283-8000.
**INDIANA UNIVERSITY SCHOOL OF MUSIC**
Technical studies, Bloomington 47405. (812) 337-1613.
**STARFOX/AUDIO REC'G INSTITUTE**
4602 Newaygo Rd., Fort Wayne 46808. (219) 483-9564. George Leinorweber.

# IOWA

**RECORDING INSTITUTE OF AMERICA
AT A&R RECORDING**
2700 Ford St., Ames 50010. (515) 232-2991.
**UNIVERSITY OF IOWA
SCHOOL OF MUSIC**
Iowa City 52242. (319) 353-5976. Lowell Cross.

# KANSAS

**KANSAS STATE UNIVERSITY
MUSIC DEPARTMENT**
Manhattan, KS 66506. (913) 532-5740. Hanley Jackson.

**RECORDING INSTITUTE OF AMERICA
AT SUNSET STUDIOS**
117 W. Eighth St., Hays 67601. (913) 625-9634. Mark Meckel.

# LOUISIANA

**RECORDING INSTITUTE OF AMERICA
AT KNIGHT RECORDING STUDIO**
3116 Metairie Rd., Metairie 70001. (504) 834-5711. Traci Borges.

# MARYLAND

**BIRCH RECORDING STUDIO**
c/o Salisbury State Coll., 113 W. Main, Secretary 21664. (301) 943-8141. Paul R. Birch.
**GOUCHER COLLEGE**
Dulaney Valley Rd., Towson 21204. (301) 337-6277. Flo Ayres.
**J R B SOUND STUDIOS**
4917 Cordell Ave., Bethesda 20014. (301) 654-2055. John Burr.
**OMEGA STUDIOS SCHOOL OF
APPLIED RECORDING ARTS & SCIENCES**
10518 Connecticut Ave., Kensington 20795. (301) 946-4686. W. Robert Yesbek.
**SHEFFIELD REC'GS LTD. INC.**
13816 Sunnybrook Rd., Phoenix 21131. (301) 628-7260. Nancy Scaggs.

# MASSACHUSETTS

**AUDIO WORKSHOP SCHOOL OF SOUND**
84 Long Ave., Belmont, MA 02178. (617) 369-1711. Steve Langstaff.

# MICHIGAN

**CLOUD BORN AUDIO SCHOOL**
18000 Mack Ave., Grosse Pointe 48224. (313) 882-0566. Ken Sands.
**RECORDING INSTITUTE OF DETROIT**
14611 E. Nine Mile, East Detroit (313) 779-1380. John Jaszcz.

# MINNESOTA

**BROWN INSTITUTE INC.**
3123 E. Lake St., Minneapolis 55406. (612) 721-2481. William Johnson.
**COOKHOUSE RECORDING STUDIO**
2541 Nicollet, Minneapolis 55404 (612) 827-5441. Tom Paske.

**MOONSOUND/McPHAIL CENTER
FOR THE ARTS**
2828 Dupont, Minneapolis 55408. (612) 824-2636. Michael Geske.

## MISSISSIPPI

**JACKSON STATE UNIVERSITY**
1325 Lynch St., Jackson 39203. (601) 968-2121.

## MISSOURI

**ST. LOUIS SCHOOL OF RECORDING**
103 Elk Run Dr., Eureka 63023. (314) 938-6566. Rich Rhiel.
**THIS BUSINESS OF MUSIC
AT OZARK OPRY RECS., INC.**
PO Box 242, Osage Beach 65065. (314) 348-2270.
**WEBSTER COLLEGE**
470 E. Lockwood, Webster Grove 63119. (314) 968-0500.

## NEBRASKA

**UNIVERSITY OF NEBRASKA AT OMAHA**
60th & Dodge, Omaha 68132. (402) 554-2200.

## NEVADA

**C S S RECORDING STUDIOS**
2010 E. Charleston, Las Vegas 89104. (702) 384-1212 Debbie Parks.
**UNIVERSITY OF NEVADA-LAS VEGAS**
4505 S. Maryland Pkwy., Las Vegas 89109. (702) 739-3011.

## NEW JERSEY

**OMNI RECORDING STUDIOS INC.**
44 Abbett Ave., Morristown 07960. (201) 539-8804. Rick Kerner.

## NEW YORK

**AUDIO REC'G TECHNOLOGY INSTITUTE**
756 Main St., Farmingdale, NY 11735. (516) 454-8999. James J. Bernard.
**CENTER FOR AUDIO STUDIES**
12 St. John St., Red Hook 12571. (914) 758-5605. David R. Moulton.
**CORNELL UNIVERSITY**
Ithaca, NY 14853. (607) 256-1000.

**EASTMAN SCHOOL OF MUSIC**
26 Gibbs St., Rochester 14604. (716) 275-3180. Ros Ritchie.
**INSTITUTE OF AUDIO RESEARCH**
64 University Pl., New York 10003. (212) 677-7580. Philip Stein, Albert B. Grundy.
**MANHATTAN SCHOOL OF MUSIC**
120 Claremont Ave., New York 10003. (212) 749-2802. Philip Stein.
**NEW SCHOOL FOR SOCIAL RESEARCH**
66 W. 12, New York 10011. (212) 925-3721. John Watts.
**NEW YORK UNIVERSITY
DEPARTMENT OF MUSIC EDUCATION**
35 W. Fourth St., Rm 777, New York 10003. (212) 598-3491. Richard Broderick.
**RECORDING CONCEPTS LTD.**
625 Panorama Trail, Rochester 14625. (716) 381-2300. Roderick (Rory) J. Williams.
**RECORDING INSTITUTE OF AMERICA**
220 Westbury Ave., Carle Place, New York 11514. (516) 334-7750. Chas Kimbrell.
**RHYTHM SECTION LAB**
130 W. 42nd St., New York, 10036. (212) 840-0433. Robert Wallis, Paul Siegal.
**ROCKLAND INSTITUTE OF RECORDING**
73 No. Main St., Spring Valley 10977. (914) 425-0018.
**SOUND HOUSE**
4 Scenic Dr., Newburgh 12550. (914) 561-1206. Donna Gamma.
**SOUND MERCHANT**
223 Broadway, Rensselaer 12144. (518) 434-2014. John Hilton.
**SOUND RECORDING TECHNOLOGY**
Mason Hall Studio, Suny, Fredonia, NY 14063. (716) 673-3151, 673-3221. David Moulton.
**STATE UNIV. OF NEW YORK
AT ALBANY**
1400 Washington Ave., Albany 12222. (518) 457-3300.
**STATE UNIV. OF NEW YORK
AT FREDONIA MUSIC DEPARTMENT**
Fredonia 14063. (716) 673-3249.
**SYRACUSE UNIVERSITY**
Syracuse 13210. (315) 423-1870.

## NORTH CAROLINA

**NORTH CAROLINA SCHOOL
OF THE ARTS**
PO Box 12189. Winston-Salem 27107. (919) 784-7170.
**RECORDING INSTITUTE OF AMERICA
AT REFLECTION STUDIOS**
1018 Central Ave., Charlotte 28204. (704) 377-4596.

## OHIO

**ALCON RECORDING STUDIOS INC.**
35100 Euclid Ave., Ste 300, Cleveland 44094.
(216) 951-0910. Kevin Collins.
**BROWNWOOD STUDIOS**
1512 C. R. 90, Gibsonburg 43431. (419) 665-
2112. R. T. Brown.
**CLEVELAND INSTITUTE OF MUSIC**
11021 East Blvd., Cleveland 44106. (216)
791-5165.
**5TH FLOOR RECORDING STUDIOS
SOUND ENGINEERING COURSE**
517 W. Third St. Cincinnati 45202. (513)
651-1871. Rich Goldman.
**JEWEL AUDIO RECORDING SCHOOL**
1594 Kinney Ave., Cincinnati 45231. (513)
522-9336. Rusty York.
**KINGSMILL RECORDING STUDIO**
1033 Kingsmill Pkwy., Columbus 43229. (614)
846-4494. Don Spangler.
**LAKELAND COMMUNITY COLLEGE**
Box 90, Mentor (216) 953-7000.
**OHIO STATE UNIVERSITY
SCHOOL OF MUSIC**
1866 College Rd., Columbus 43210. (614)
422-6508. Dr. David L. Meeker.
**RECORDING INSTITUTE OF AMERICA
AT MUS-I-COL RECORDING STUDIOS**
780 Oakland Park Ave., Columbus 43224.
(614) 267-3133. Terry Douds.
**RECORDING INSTITUTE OF AMERICA**
1730 E. 24 St., Cleveland 44114. (216) 621-
0810.
**RECORDING WORKSHOP**
455 Massieville Rd., Chillicothe 45601. (614)
663-2544. James Rosebrook.

## OKLAHOMA

**SUNSET WEST RECORDING**
1448 N. Harvard, Tulsa 74115. (918) 936-
4109. Chris Hollis.

## OREGON

**RECORDING ASSOCS.**
5821 SE Powell Blvd., Portland 97206. (503)
777-4621. Jay Webster.
**REX RECORDING CO.**
1931 SE Morrison, Portland 97214. (503) 238-
4525. Russell E. Gorsline.

## PENNSYLVANIA

**AMERICAN ARTIST STUDIO**
PO Box 131, Erie 16512. (814) 455-4796. Skip
Niebauer.
**LEBANON VALLEY COLLEGE**
Annville 17003. (717) 867-4411.
**JON MILLER SCHOOL FOR
RECORDING ARTS & SCIENCES**
2524 E. Scenic Dr., Bath 18014. (215) 837-
7550. Jon Miller.
**PENNSYLVANIA STATE UNIVERSITY**
UniversityPark 16802. (814) 865-4700.
**RECORDING INSTITUTE OF AMERICA
AT AUDIO INNOVATORS INC.**
216 Blvd. of the Allies, Pittsburgh 15222.
(412) 471-4777. Gary Popotnick.
**RECORDING INSTITUTE OF AMERICA
AT STARR RECORDING INC.**
200 St. James Pl, Philadelphia 19106. (215)
925-5265. Rose Payne.
**YORK COLLEGE OF PENNSYLVANIA**
Country Club Rd. York 17405. (717) 846-
7788.

## RHODE ISLAND

**BROWN UNIVERSITY**
54 College St., Providence 02912. (401) 863-
1000.
**NORMANDY SOUND INC.**
25 Market St., Warren 02885. (401) 247-0218.
**UNIVERSITY OF RHODE ISLAND**
Kingston 02881 (401) 792-1000.

## SOUTH CAROLINA

**MASTERPIECE RECORDING STUDIO**
4478 Ft. Jackson Blvd., Columbia 29209.
(803) 787-8360. Joel Johnson.
**M C P/DAVISOUND**
PO Box 521, Newberry 29108. (801) 276-
0639. Polly Davis.
**RECORDING INSTITUTE OF AMERICA
AT THE SOUNDING BOARD**
PO Box 888, Hwy 153, Easley 29640 (803)
269-7012. Otis Forrest.

## TENNESSEE

**BELMONT COLLEGE
MUSIC BUSINESS DIVISION**
Nashville 37203. (615) 383-7001, X 206. Dr.
Jay Collins, Director.

**GEORGE PEABODY COLLEGE**
**MUSIC DEPARTMENT**
21 Ave. S., Nashville 37203. (615) 327-8121.
**HILLSBORO RECORDING PROGRAM**
Hillsboro High School, 3812 Hillsboro Rd.,
Nashville 37215. (615) 383-5511. Vic Gabany.
**MIDDLE TENNESSEE STATE UNIV.**
**MUSIC DEPARTMENT**
Murfreesboro 37132. (615) 898-2813. Geoffrey Hull.
**NASHVILLE STUDIO THEATRE/TIME**
**INSTITUTE**
1302 Division, Nashville 37203 (615) 242-1650. C.L. Roberson.
**THUNDERHEAD SOUND STUDIOS**
112 17 St., Knoxville 37916. (615) 546-8006.
D. Wayne Goforth.
**UNIVERSITY OF TENNESSEE**
**MUSIC DEPARTMENT**
1741 Volunteer Blvd., Knoxville 37916. (615)
974-5489, 974-3241. Dr. Kenneth Jacobs.

## TEXAS

**SKIP FRAZEE AUDIO ENG. SCHOOL**
c/o January Sound Studios, 3341 Towerwood,
Dallas 75234. (214) 243-3735 Les Studdard.
**NORTH TEXAS STATE UNIVERSITY**
PO Box 13887, Denton 76203. (817) 788-2521.
**PRODUCTION HOUSE**
Box 31767, Dallas 75231. (214) 661-3346. Bob
Freeman.
**RECORDING INSTITUTE OF AMERICA**
**AT WELLS SOUND STUDIO**
2036 Pasket, Houston 77092. (713) 688-8067.
Barbara Pennington.
**SAN ANTONIO COLLEGE**
**DEPT. OF RADIO-TV-FILM**
1300 San Pedro Ave., San Antonio 78284.
(512) 733-2793. Jean M. Longwith.
**TEXAS MUSIC ARTS COLLEGE**
8375 Westview, Houston 77055. (713) 465-6554. Dale Mullins.
**TRINITY UNIVERSITY**
**DEPT. OF COMMUNICATIONS**
715 Stadium Dr., San Antonio 78284. (512)
736-8113.

## UTAH

**BRIGHAM YOUNG UNIVERSITY**
**DEPARTMENT OF MUSIC**
C-550 Harris Fine Arts Center, Provo 84602.
(801) 374-1211 X 3083. Dr. A. Harold Goodman.

## VERMONT

**RECORDING INSTITUTE OF AMERICA**
**AT STARBUCK/ASHLEY RECORDING**
**STUDIOS INC.**
77 College St., Burlington 05401 (802) 658-4616. Mark Ashley.

## VIRGINIA

**NORTHERN VIRGINIA COMMUNITY**
**COLLEGE/LOUDOUN CAMPUS**
1000 Harry F. Byrd Hwy., Sterling 22170.
(703) 323-4507, 323-4527. Bob Miller.
**RECORDING INSTITUTE OF AMERICA**
**AT ALPHA AUDIO**
2049 W. Broad St., Richmond 23220. (804)
358-3852. Eric. Johnson.

## WASHINGTON

**AAA/TRIANGLE RECORDING STUDIO**
4230 Leary Way, NW, Seattle 98107. (206)
783-3869. William Stuber.
**KEARNEY BARTON'S AUDIO**
**RECORDING SCHOOL**
2227 Fifth Ave., Seattle 98121. (206) 623-2030. Kearney W. Barton.
**EASTERN WASHINGTON UNIV.**
Cheney 99004. (509) 359-2228. Dr. Ray L.
Barnes.
**EVERGREEN STATE COLLEGE**
Communications Bldg., Evergreen State College, Olympia 98505. (206) 866-6096. Dave
Englert, Ken Wilhelm.
**HOLDEN, HAMILTON & ROBERTS INC.**
2227 N. 56th, Seattle 98103. (206) 632-8300.
Lanita De Mers, Coy Owen.
**RECORDING INSTITUTE OF AMERICA AT**
**HOLDEN, HAMILTON & ROBERTS INC.**
2227 N. 56 St., Seattle 98103. (206) 632-8300. Herb R. Hamilton, Jr.

## WEST VIRGINIA

**SWEETSONG RECORDING**
PO Box 2041, Parkersburg 26101. (304) 489-2911. Roger Hoover.

## WISCONSIN

**DAVE KENNEDY RECORDING**
231 W.Wisconsin Ave., Milwaukee 52303.
(414) 273-5720. Jim Autz.

# MUSIC RELATED ORGANIZATIONS

**A G A C (American Guild of Authors and Composers),** 40 W. 57th St., New York, N.Y. 10019. (212) 757-8833. "AGAC/The Songwriter's Guild is the only 50 year old national organization run by and for songwriters for the purpose of furthering and protecting their rights in the music business."

**A F of M (American Federation of Musicians),** 1500 Broadway, New York, N.Y. 10036. (212) 869-1330.

**A F T R A (American Federation of Television and Radio Artists),** Becker & London, 15 Columbus Circle, New York, N.Y. 10023. (212) 265-7700.

**L.A. Songwriters Showcase,** 6772 Hollywood Blvd., Hollywood, CA 90028. (213) 462-1382. "A non-profit songwriter service organization that includes an annual songwriter expo, educational programs, and showcasing to the music industry through both live and taped mediums."

**Musicians Contact Service,** 6605 Sunset Blvd., Hollywood, CA 90028. (213) 467-2191.

**Professional Musicians Career Academy,** 3040 Lyndale Ave. S., Minneapolis, MN 55408, (612) 827-5791, (a subsidiary of Boyd Hunt Enterprises). "Provides workshops for professional musicians, including step-by-step career direction, methods for development and assembly of musical material, training and preparation for recording, and training and opportunities to develop careers in music related areas other than performance."

**PMR (Professional Musicians Referral)** (a subsidiary of Boyd Hunt Enterprises). "Maintains the largest listings of individual musicians seeking groups and groups seeking new members."
**Main Offices:** 3150 Lyndale Ave. S., Minneapolis, MN 55408. (800) 328-8660 or (612) 825-6848 for Minnesota residents.
**West Coast Office:** 8761 Katella Ave., Anaheim, CA 92804. (714) 527-5611.
**East Coast Office:** 106 White Horse Pike, Haddon Heights, N.J. 08035. (609) 547-7096.

**S R S (Songwriter Resources and Services),** 6772 Hollywood Blvd., Hollywood, CA 90028. (213) 463-7178. "Dedicated to the education and protection of songwriters and fosters the art and craft of American song writing."

---

"Finally there is a book that covers the whole music business. It's easy reading, easy to understand and truly encouraging. The book saves me a lot of talking. I now tell my friends, "Don't leave without it."
—Paul Leka, *(Producer of REO, Harry Chapin, Gloria Gaynor, and others)*

"I have been in the music business for over fifteen years. The book really held my interest. It's fantastic, very informative, and highly entertaining."
—Jim Paris, *(Producer of Buddy Midles)*

"I'd recommend the book to any musician looking for either platinum or gold at the end of the rainbow."
—Lew Irwin, *(Earth News)*

"A wonderful introduction to the inside working of the music business. It's concise, enjoyable and practical. My students rave about it.
—Ted Stern, *Instructor, Commercial Music, Glendale Community College, Glendale, Calif.*

"Your wealth of information along with a delightfully lively writing style make for easy reading and more important, easy to retain. Your book, The Platinum Rainbow, is now my textbook for my course in Music As A Business."
—Alan Remington, *Prof. of Music, Orange Coast College, Costa Mesa, CA.*

"Anyone who even slightly desires a career in the music industry must read this book! The information is straighforward, honest, and written in an entertaining manner."
—Dr. Rodney Oaks, *Composer, Director of Electronic Music Studios, Los Angeles Harbor College, Wilmington, CA*

"The Platinum Rainbow is the best book of its kind...our students use it over and over, again and again."
—Gerry Schroeder, *Co-chaiman, Commercial Music,. Golden West College, Huntington Beach, CA*

"Every serious music industry person should read this book. Struggling amateurs, because it will help you to many things you need to know. Successful pros, because it will confirm what you already know and give you plenty of laughs."
—Dr. George Shaw, *Coordinator of Commercial Music, Long Beach City College, Long Beach, CA*

"After 20 years as a music educator I learned a tremendous amount about the business of music."
—Gerald R. Eskelin, *L.A. Jazz Choir; Music Chairman, L.A. Pierce College, Woodland Hills, CA*

# What the Music Business is Saying

"Buy *two* copies of this book—one will be an invaluable reference on your way to the top of the music business; the other will help you keep your feet on the ground after you have made it to the top (and in the process you probably threw away the first copy)."
—Bones Howe *(Producer of Tom Waits, The Association, The Turtles, The 5th Dimension and many others.)*

"At this moment, The Platinum Rainbow is the *definitive* book about the music/record business. It's often humorous, at times brutal, extremely informative, and always honest. Always."
—Dick La Palm, *The Village Recorder*

"Without a doubt, the best book on the real music business."
—Shelly Weiss, *Manager of Sneaker and Publisher (Sneaker Songs, Shell Sounds)*

"The Platinum Rainbow is undoubtedly the most comprehensive and yet witty introductory guide to the ins and outs of the music business. Whether one is a fledgling song writer or veteran industry executive or anything in-between, I highly recommend it."
—Andrew Stern *(Attorney at Law)*

"Bob Monaco and James Riordan are two candidly honest and sincere people who obviously know the music business from its pitfalls to its successes. The Platinum Rainbow offers those truths to be found by each and every one of us who truly believe. A source of inspiration to those of us who have been stepped on by the big music machine."
—Sal Marquez *(Composer, arranger, producer, recording artist with Frank Zappa & The Mothers, The Beach Boys, Helena Springs, Woody Herman and Buddy Rich)*

An informative, useful yet easy-to-read account of the music business. It is worthwhile reading."
—Neil Portnow, *Vice Pres., A&R-West Coast, Arista Records*

"Too much information has been disseminated about this business, but now the *first and most practical* approach to the recording industry has been written. Authored by seasoned pros, it is a must for knowing what the music business is all about."
—Jay S. Lowy, *V.P. & General Manager, Jobete Music Co., Inc., Former Pres. of NARAS*

"For all Rock and Roll survivors, The Platinum Rainbow is the set list for the Greatest Concert you'll ever perform. This book is for the next wave of Creative Artists, a virtual road-map—street, avenue, and alley."
—Marty McCann, *Peavey Electronics Corp.*

"I recommend this book to anyone seeking an honest, realistic view of what the record industry is all about."
—Rick Christian *(Composer of many songs, including "I Don't Need You" by Kenny Rogers)*

"A 'must read' for anyone who wants a complete overview of the music and record industry. The Platinum Rainbow covers more ground that any book of its kind."
—Eddie Lambert, *Vice President, Creative Activities, 20th Century Fox Music Group*

"Very enlightening. I wish it had been there when I started out."
—Sylvia Shemwell *(Former member of The Sweet Inspirations and Elvis Presley Show)*

"A book with the quality of the Platinum Rainbow has been long overdue. Should be a required prerequisite for anyone who is serious about getting into a career in music."
—Bruce Lowe, *(L.A. Session Musician and Producer)*

"Not only is this book a valuable educational guide but it is very entertaining. The most readable book ever written on the music business."
—Denis Degher, *Engineer and Producer*

# What Radio and Television are Saying

"'By sharing their practical and realistic insights into the working of the music business, Riordan and Monaco have performed a much needed service to not only aspiring newcomers, but to the actual industry itself.''

—Mike Harrison, *KMET Los Angeles*

"For the first time a book is available that literally tells you the truth about the music business. You ought to read it, it's the bible.''

—Roy Leonard, *WGN Chicago*

"It's how to do it the right way. The authors have all the credentials and it's all in this book.''

—Regis Philbin, *A.M. Los Angeles*

"Obviously the music disciples of L.A., Bob Monaco and James Riordan, journeyed to the sacred Rock on which rock and roll was founded, because they have written *the* inspired book of revelations about how to survive in the music business without losing your "zen-ses.''

—Cherie Sannes, *KRTH Los Angeles*

"If you're interested in the business, go out and pick up a copy. It is a step by step guide and believe me it has lots of information.''

—Regina Hayes, *WLS Chicago*

# THE PLATINUM RAINBOW CASSETTE SERIES

*This instructional cassette series features "PLATINUM RAINBOW" authors Bob Monaco and James Riordan discussing a variety of career opportunities within the music business. Many top industry professionals also appear on the tapes to discuss their areas of expertise with Bob and James. The conversations are spiced with humor and interesting anecdotes about succeeding in the music world. The cassettes vary in length, but generally run about forty-five minutes. Please designate tape number when ordering.*

TAPE #                                                                SUBJECT

101  **SONGWRITING,** lyrics and melody, collaboration, hooks, arrangement and production, songwriting competitions, taking an organized approach, demos, commercial songwriting, shopping your songs.

102  **PUBLISHING.** The role of a publisher, what a publisher looks for in a songwriter, what a songwriter should look for in a publisher, recording and packaging the demo, contracts, international publishing, protecting songs, self publishing, becoming a publisher, contacting publishers.

103  **RECORD PRODUCTION.** Producers role, choosing a producer, what does a producer look for in an artist, staff/independent producers, engineers, picking a studio, mixing and mastering, shoping a deal.

104  **RECORD ENGINEERING.** Engineer's role, becoming an engineer, what an artist should look for in an engineer, audio/film/video engineering, studio managing, engineer/producers, advances in audio technology, starting your own studio.

105  **MUSIC LAW.** When you need an attorney, picking the right one, major points of a recording contract, publishing contracts, paying an attorney, copyright law, becoming a music attorney, the statuatory rate law and record labels, attorneys shopping deals.

106  **CAREERS IN RADIO.** Becoming a deejay, air personalities, women in radio, career opportunities, automation, radio formats, ratings, satellite and cable radio, video deejays, getting records on the radio.

107  **PROFESSIONAL ATTITUDE.** Realizing your limitations, goal setting, making a decision, having a leader, kicking your brother out of the band, not advertising you're an idiot, the myths of the music business, fear and greed.

108  **MANAGERS AND AGENTS.** What they do, picking the right one, dealing with them, becoming a manager or agent, when you need one, getting gigs, press kits, little league agents, being your own manager, managers and agents shopping a deal.

**ONLY $9.95 EACH**

***ORDER THE ENTIRE SERIES OF EIGHT CASSETTES FOR ONLY $69.95***

**Swordsman Press**, 15445 Ventura Bl., St. 10
Sherman Oaks, California 91413

☐ Please send me the following cassettes _____
_____ Total Enclosed $_____
(Cal. res. add 40¢ per tape sales tax) Please encl. $1.50 for postage & handling.
Visa or MasterCard No. _____

Name _____
Address _____
City/State/Zip_____

# What the Press is Saying

"If you want to learn 'How To Succeed In The Music Business Without Selling Your Soul' read The Platinum Rainbow."

*—Chicago Tribune*

"It isn't likely we'll see a better how-to book for some time."

*—Daily News*

"Details in a conversational tone on how to succeed in the music business. Written with a sense of of humor, the book offers solid advice."

*—Record World*

"Steers prospective musicians clear of all the myths, red tape and sidetracking associated with getting a music career off the ground."

*—The Tribune, Phoenix, Ariz.*

"Is the next most difficult thing to getting a hit record keeping a firm grip on morals? Read The Platinum Rainbow!"

*—Las Vegas Sun*

"A Step-by-step guide for making it in the music industry."

*—Minneapolis Tribune*

"Plenty of factual savvy and no-bull info. A blow by blow breakdown of the ins and outs of the music biz."

*—The Aquarian, New York, N.Y.*

"It's everything you always wanted to know about the music business but didn't know who to ask."

*—Indianapolis News*

"We very highly recommend a wonderful book on the entertainment world. It's called The Platinum Rainbow.

*—Soul Magazine*

"A commendable job of presenting the ins and outs of succeeding in the music business."

*—Guitar Player Magazine*

"The Platinum Rainbow is the first insightful and streetwise instruction manual for understanding the music industry . . . that also happens to be fun to read."

*—David Schwartz Editor/Publisher Mix Magazine*

"Packed with so much inside information I felt I had discovered a secret initiation manual misplaced by one of the high priests of the music business. The authors are definitely insiders who happen to care enough about creative people and the music they make to give us all the real inside scoop on the ground rules of making records."

*—S.R.S. Newsletter (Songwriter's Resources and Services)*

"The ultimate career book on the music business."

*—Recording Engineer and Producer*

"An oasis in a vast desert of over-hip, over-hyped, and myth-obsessed books on the music business. Highly recommended for anyone serious about music as a career."

*—Music Connection*

"Thoroughly stimulating reading. The closest thing yet to a do-it-yourself treatise on how to succeed in the music business without selling your soul. Exposes true nature of music business.

*—Illinois Entertainer*

"The book takes the reader through just about every aspect of the music business including both the creative and business angles. Monaco and Riordan have a nice conversational writing style and more importantly *they know what they are talking about!*"

*—John Mankiewicz. Los Angeles Herald Examiner*

## If you want to be a success in the music business without selling your soul,

*The Platinum Rainbow,* a new book by Grammy award winning record producer
Bob Monaco and nationally syndicated music columnist James Riordan,
will give you an inside look at the recording industry and tell you how to think realistically
in a business based on fantasy, how to promote yourself, how to get a manager,
producer or agent, how to get free recording time, how to make a deal, how to recognize
and record a hit song, how to be a session musician, how to kick your brother
out of the band, how to put together the six key elements a record company looks for.

*The Platinum Rainbow,* over 200 pages, quotes some of the biggest names in pop music
and gives you a complete analysis of The Song; The Studio; The Stage; Demo
Or Master; Cutting A Record; Hooks And Arrangements; The Producer; The Engineer;
The Budget; The Basic Track; Vocals; Overdubs; The Mix; The 24 Track Monster;
Things You Can Hear But Can't See; The Deal; The Creative Businessman; The Music Attorney;
The Manager, Agent, Promoter; The Artist As Vendor; Leverage, Clout And The
Ladder; Getting A Job With A Record Company; Gigs; The Golden Reel To Reel
And The Platinum Turntable; Staying Happy; Waiting To Be Discovered And
Nine Other Popular Myths About The Music Business.

*The Platinum Rainbow* also includes a complete DIRECTORY of record companies,
producers, managers, publishers, agents, studios, engineering schools, concert promoters,
all the names, addresses, phone numbers of who to contact. The music business
is not mysterious and it is not magical. The music business is a game, and like any game,
it has its own set of rules. Once you know the rules, you can decide if you want to play.
If you do, *The Platinum Rainbow* will show you how to give it your best shot,
and if you are not happy with the knowledge this book gives you,
return it within two weeks and we will send you your money back.